M000085549

What People Are Saying About
Still Off-Base About Race

"In this timely volume, Dr. Michael Reynolds offers a gift to the Christian community struggling with the current racial tensions in the USA and abroad. Establishing the fact that race is not based in biology or genetics but is a social construct that stands in contrast to a biblical understanding, Reynolds offers a helpful, though painful, survey of the African American experience as the context by which to move forward in a way befitting the body of Christ. It is a primer for the church in these challenging days, a primer the church ignores at its own peril."

—John Christopher Thomas Ph.D., University of Sheffield, Clarence J. Abbott Professor of Biblical Studies, Pentecostal Theological Seminary, Director of the Centre for Pentecostal and Charismatic Studies, Bangor University, Wales

"Dr. Michael Reynolds, director of Ministerial Development for the Church of God, has written a timely book titled, *Still Off-Base About Race*. While the book gives a historical account of long-term issues, more importantly it addresses the concerns that face the church and the world, as well as giving redemptive answers to the questions about race. The experiences illustrated by Dr. Reynolds give us an opportunity to discuss these issues and bring us together. It is time for the church to address these matters of faith and community, and then seek to answer them from a Christ-centered and redemptive faith."

—Dr. Tim Hill, General Overseer, Church of God , Cleveland, Tennessee

"The Church of God as a movement is indebted to the leadership Dr. Michael D. Reynolds has brought to the office of Ministerial Development in the 21st century. His rich background of serving in the forefront of ministry as lead pastor of New Life Celebration Church of God in Dolton, Illinois, for more than 28 years and his service in the following positions—professor, executive director, and dean at Trinity for more than 25 years—allow him the unique ability to address one of our culture's biggest challenges today: the race issue.

"As a recognized speaker, Dr. Reynolds has conducted global seminars on the topic of race. He is now providing a well-researched, academic, and pastoral view on race that is salvific and healthy to the body of Christ.

"*Still Off-Base About Race* is not like any other book on race today. It is a must-read and a resource for ministry leaders and laity. The truth discussed in this book provides a pathway to healing for the divided church and world cultures."

—*Dr. David Ramírez, Third Assistant*
General Overseer, Church of God

"Dr. Reynolds has given a scholarly approach to understanding the nuances of our own humanity. Masterfully weaving together sociology, biology, and an academic look at race is certainly the missing ingredient for the much needed harmony among all people. The Bible says, "In all your getting get understanding" (Proverbs 4:7, NKJV). Dr. Reynolds has mastered the art of leading us toward a greater understanding of race. As a senior pastor, this book is unquestionably a dynamic resource for teaching and training my leadership and congregation. I would be selling this book and Dr. Reynolds short by simply saying, 'It's genius—it's divinely inspired!'"

—*Pastor Smokie Norful, Victory Cathedral*
Worship Center, Bolingbrook, Illinois

STILL

OFF-BASE

WHEN WE KNOW THE TRUTH, THINGS WILL BE DIFFERENT

ABOUT

RACE

DR. MICHAEL REYNOLDS

**DREAM
RELEASER**
ENTERPRISES

For foreign and subsidiary rights, contact the author.

Cover design by: Joe De Leon

ISBN: 978-1-954089-17-4   1 2 3 4 5 6 7 8 9 10

Printed in the United States of America

DEDICATION

I dedicate this book to my beautiful wife, Erica,
who walks in love and follows Christ.
I also dedicate this book to my four children:
Michael, Celenna, Jonathan, and Cicely—
And my four beautiful grandchildren—
Michael III, Chloe, Eric, and Levi.

"And he made from one man every nation of mankind to
live on all the face of the earth, having determined allotted periods
and the boundaries of their dwelling place" (Acts 17:26).

"A new commandment I give to you, that you love one another: just
as I have loved you, you also are to love one another" (John 13:34).

FOREWORD

In *Still Off-Base About Race: When We Know the Truth, Things Will Be Different*, Michael Reynolds brings his experience as a university professor, seminary associate dean, and leading Pentecostal pastor to the conversation about race, with which the United States as a country is having difficulty engaging. Along with race being addressed by best-selling books, award-winning televised interviews, mesmerizing viral sermons, and paradigm-shifting lectures, this clearly written and easy-to-read book seeks to take race seriously as a topic the church must tackle.

Within this fine book, Reynolds displays his ability to weave biology, sociology, anthropology, history, Scripture, and theology along with gripping moments from his autobiography into his insightful analysis of race as a critical topic offers stunning insight into race as a pressing problem that harms the church and society. While African Americans are the primary focus of this important book, Reynolds also discusses the plight of the First Peoples or Native Americans. In addition to analyzing racism and offering a spectrum of racial practices that categorize different racial behaviors, Reynolds provides lucid ways to envision the church and society marked by racial justice.

Reynolds shows in the book how racism can tear away at the social fabric of congregations and countries along with maiming and killing black people. For Reynolds, a solid education about race can dispel racial ignorance and change racial attitudes and behaviors. He thoughtfully educates readers about crucial distinctions between prejudice and structural racism, for instance. Acknowledging that education alone is insufficient in eradicating racism, he recognizes the vital role of social activism. In *Still Off-Base About Race*, the reader encounters the heroic efforts of African American activists such as

W. E. B. Du Bois, Fannie Lou Hamer, and Martin Luther King Jr., as well as White American activists such as Viola Liuzzo and Jonathan Daniels; these Christians of both races are noted as history-makers. As champions of the Civil Rights Movement who risked their lives and some lost their lives in dismantling racist structures and erecting structures of racial justice, they are stellar witnesses to God's vision of humanity. In addition, Reynolds illustrates the essential role that constructive interracial relationships can play in unlearning the microaggression of racism. According to Reynolds, it will take a multifaceted engagement of race to end racism.

While *Still Off-Base About Race* is a fascinating interdisciplinary book, it is a Christian book which takes theology very seriously. For Reynolds, Pentecost defines an inaugural moment when the Holy Spirit reconciles people who had been separated by racism, overturning the division that grew out of the Tower of Babel, and anticipating the vision of John in Revelation about heaven as a place with people from every tribe, nation, and language. Theology is really interwoven throughout the book. Throughout this text, Reynolds demonstrates his talents as a Christian scholar.

As a friend of nearly three decades and a former professor of Dr. Michael Reynolds, I have learned from his scholarly work, pastoral leadership, collegiality, and now, this book. I invite the reader to join me in being taught by him and, as a consequence, to discover more about God's vision for humanity and a world without racism.

Still Off-Base About Race offers pastors and laypeople a great resource to live in God's vision of the church of all races and a just society. May committed Christians intelligently and prayerfully enter the conversation that Michael Reynolds has so graciously framed for the church.

—Dr. David D. Daniels III
Henry Winters Luce Professor of World Christianity
McCormick Theological Seminary
Chicago, Illinois

ACKNOWLEDGMENTS

A published work is never the work of a single individual but always the culmination of skilled craftsmen who work together to produce a quality book for the readers.

- » I commend, my copyeditor, Nellie Keasling, for her diligence in bringing the manuscript to final fulfillment.
- » I must also recognize the love and support of my wife, Erica, and my children—Michael Reynolds II, Celenna Logans, Jonathan Reynolds, and Cicely Reynolds—who stood by me in this endeavor.
- » Finally, I must not fail to acknowledge the influence of the Holy Spirit whose presence daily encourages me to be "strong in the Lord and in the strength of His might" (Ephesians 6:10).

—Michael Reynolds

TABLE OF CONTENTS

Introduction:
Class Is in Session

I'm guessing you picked up this book because you're concerned about the number and degree of racial injustices in recent weeks and months. Black communities, with increasing African support, are becoming more vocal about seeing something done. With the media spotlight on recent killings of Black people by white police officers, it has been impossible to ignore the growing tension. We have all learned the names of many of those Black victims: Trayvon Martin, Michael Brown, Eric Garner, Breonna Taylor, George Floyd, and too many more. Yet as I write this, CBS News has recently listed the names of 164 Black people killed by police between January 1 and August 31, 2020. That includes at least one death every week and involves every state except Rhode Island and Vermont.[1] And by the time this book gets published, I fear the list will be considerably longer.

We all want answers. We want solutions. Yet as evident as the problem has become, the resolution is not a quick or simple one. As I will remind you in this book, the inequality between Blacks and whites began even before our country was founded and has continued throughout every decade since. If we really want to resolve the problems that arise from race, we first need to consider how those problems were created in the first place.

I know many people are eager to jump right to solutions and strategies for better racial harmony and interaction, but I hope you will be willing to slow down a bit. Rather than addressing race from the

---

1   "Police in the U.S. Killed 164 Black People in the First 8 Months of 2020. These Are Their Names," CBS News, https://www.cbsnews.com/pictures/black-people-killed-by-police-in-the-u-s-in-2020/.

top down, I will be approaching it from the bottom up. We need to get to the roots. We need to see where the feelings come from, and how hatred can develop. It is my strong and long-held belief that before we are able to arrive at any lasting and workable solutions to problems arising from race, we must first develop a much broader and deeper understanding of how those problems originated.

I teach a class called "What Is Race?" and I will be sharing much of that content with you throughout this book. Racial issues affect more areas of our lives than many of us realize. In fact, I have organized my thoughts around several relevant topics, and as you go through them, it may feel as if you are moving from class to class on a school day.

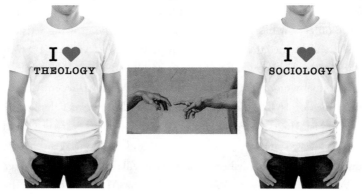

We are going to start with some biology and sociology; we will spend a great deal of time in history and even take a short course—as referenced in the picture above—on theology. Eventually, we will arrive at what I believe are some workable solutions to address the racial tension that so many of us are feeling.

Let me start with a disclaimer: The enormity of this topic does not allow me to address every event and every issue. We will have to leave out much more than we include. For example, most people interested in the topic will already have a good working knowledge of what is happening currently, so I did not try to address the Black Lives Matter controversy and similar recent movements. By the time a book goes to press, those "current" events would already be dated. And even though I devoted five chapters to the historic struggles concerning race, there was no possible way to cover it all. If much of this is new to you, you will need to consider this book an introduction to the topic and continue to read up on the subject on your own. (You will find no shortage of fascinating and informative material.)

Additionally, since "race" is such a broad topic, I made no attempt to include all ethnicities. Unfortunately, a book this size cannot adequately cover the histories and problems of all the groups typically classified by race, so I will focus primarily on my own culture— African American. Most minority ethnic groups have had similar disturbing and distressing histories and can relate to oppression at the hands of those who are more populous and powerful. In its long and sometimes inglorious history, the United States government has at times demonstrated despicable and inhuman treatment toward not only people of African descent but also Native Americans, numerous Latino and Asian groups, and others. Our stories are discrete and distinctive, but we are very much alike in our suffering.

Still, I hope you will find this book not only informative, but also encouraging. As an African American, I certainly share the confusion, frustration, and anger felt by so many other African American people who are still treated like second-class citizens even today. Yet I am approaching the subject of race from a pastor's perspective, so I try to remind myself (and the reader) to approach the topic with a mindset of love, hope, forgiveness, and grace.

Too much harm has already been done in the struggle over race. I urge you to get a better understanding of the truth about race, commit to positive change wherever possible, and work together to begin to make this world a better place.

Why are we still off-base about race? Let's find out.

—Michael D. Reynolds
mreynolds@churchofgod.org
I welcome your comments about this book.

1

Eight Billion Siblings
(Biology)

The following incident happened when I was pastor of a church in the suburbs just outside Chicago. One day our church received a call from a fellow pastor who was traveling through from Mississippi whose car had broken down nearby in one of the predominantly Black neighborhoods. The deacon who took the call came in to tell me that this pastor was with his whole family, so he had looked up a local church from his denomination to get some help and advice. Since the family was involved, I assumed there would be a lot of luggage and other items they would not want to leave in a disabled car. We were preparing for our Wednesday night Bible study, so I sent out four of our church's largest men to help.

I would not find out until later that I had generated quite a startling surprise for the pastor from Mississippi. You see, in the United States, the great majority of the churches in our denomination are white, including the church of the man we were helping. Since my church was in the Chicago suburbs rather than the inner city, he was more than a little startled to see four enormous Black men come rolling up and approach his family on the side of the road. But our members brought the pastor and his family back to the church to arrange to have their car towed. They were then planning to find a hotel, but by then it was very late at night, so I insisted they stay with me and my family.

The next day the Mississippi pastor discovered that his car problem was worse than anticipated—the engine was shot and would have to be replaced. The overnight stay became almost a week-long visit. Then, when he got the bill for the car repair, it was more than he could pay. He contacted his home church, but they were reluctant to wire the money, so I assured him our church would take care of it. I could sense he was from a struggling church, and although it was a hefty amount, I thought it was the right thing to do to help out a fellow minister.

After the car repair, just as his family was preparing to leave, he asked me, "Can I tell you a story?"

I said, "Sure."

He said, "Can we take a walk?"

He and I started walking through my neighborhood. Without warning, he reached out and put his arm around me. Now, I'm a decent-sized guy, but this pastor was about six-foot-five, 350 pounds, and I was totally swallowed up by him. I don't think he realized how tight he was holding me. It was clearly an emotional moment for him. He confessed, "I am the son and grandson of KKK members, and I grew up wearing their garments. But I came to Christ, and when I did, I thought I had totally voided myself of all the issues regarding racism. I thought I had it resolved. I wasn't going around making statements. I dealt with the way I thought about others. But until I got to come here, I didn't realize how little I actually knew. I'd never spent the night in an African American person's home. I'd never shared a meal they had cooked. Everything that happened to me here would be considered vile by my family—and by me, in my past life. They would be horrified to think that I stayed with you, ate with you, went to church with you, and depended on you to take care of my car. But you have treated me better than my own church treated me. Sincerely, you're a brother; I believe you cracked the final phases of what was still holding me from transcending beyond what I used to be. And I don't think I would have gotten there had it not been for this experience with you."

We cried together for a few minutes, held each other for a moment, and then walked back to his car. He got in, rolled down the window, and added, "Do you know what I *want* to say to you? I really want to invite you to come to Mississippi and preach for me. But you can't. All of this has made me realize how much my white world is still intact. You could never come to preach from my pulpit. I don't mean any insult by that, but I feel wrong not asking you. However, I do hope we can have some kind of continuing relationship."

APPROACHING THE TOPIC OF RACE

Unless you have found some way to go completely off the grid, separated from all mass communication, internet access, and most other human beings, you have probably been hearing a great deal about the issue of race in our nation and world lately. And much of what you have heard has been disturbing. It is not like we haven't tried to heal the wounds that have accumulated from centuries of racial strife—indeed we have marched, picketed, and protested. We have debated, desegregated, and legislated. Yet, most people are still frustrated with the state of racial inequality today. Others think they have come to grips with the reality of racial differences . . . but they might be just as clueless as my Mississippi pastor friend because they have never truly been confronted with it.

WHAT RACE IS NOT

When it comes to race, it is frequently too easy and/or convenient to make assumptions about what it is. For many, it is one of those "I know it when I see it" issues. The problem is . . . that is not necessarily true. What we see and identify as racial differences may not be correct.

As we approach the topic of race, we should start with some biological truths to help bolster our understanding. Many people attempt to use biology to explain race, but their conclusions are not always accurate or credible. They do a bit of observation and determine, "Race is something that people are born into. It's the way we were created" (or perhaps the way evolution made us). But biology tells us a different story. A genetic analysis affirms that the world is made up of people who are much more alike than they could ever imagine.

Maybe you have seen detective shows where the suspect's DNA has been left at the crime scene, so the detectives send it to the lab and are told that the suspect is, let's say, an African American. When that happens, you need to remind yourself, "This is just a TV show." The fact is: *Genetics can detect no difference in a person's blood or physical makeup that credibly differentiates them by race.* A recent study by Stanford scientists concluded:

> There is no evidence that the groups we commonly call "races" have distinct, unifying genetic identities. In fact, there is ample variation within races. Ultimately, there is so much ambiguity between the races, and so much variation within them, that two people of European descent may be more genetically similar to an Asian person than they are to each other.[2]

Assumptions are often made that because we share DNA markers with people who are from a certain geographical part of the world, we can therefore infer the race of a person. However, there is nothing in your blood or saliva or elsewhere in your body system that can determine race. Race has nothing to do with nationality or ethnicity.

That fact leads us to a second truth: Because it is not a biological reality, *race then is only a humanly contrived concept.* People came up with the concept of race. They saw different skin colorings and facial

---

2   Vivian Chou, "How Science and Genetics Are Reshaping the Race Debate of the 21st Century," *Science in the News*, Harvard University Graduate School of Arts and Sciences, April 17, 2017, http://sitn.hms.harvard.edu/flash/2017/science-genetics-reshaping-race-debate-21st-century/.

features, and then they inferred differences—sometimes incredibly vast differences—that did not really exist. Essentially, race was created because one group of people wanted to find a way to feel superior, and that one group did so by making another group of people feel inferior just because they looked a little different. And over time, some groups of people began to subjugate other groups, convinced that race gave them the right to control those groups. Before we knew about DNA, people could presume that race was biological. But the reality is, that presumption cannot be justified. It just is not true.

That leads to a third point: *The definition of race changes over time.* Future chapters will show how the original beliefs about race were formed and how quickly those perceptions changed. As various cultures continued to define race in terms of color, those changes came quickly, often revolving around the need for one group to maintain economic and social power.

For instance, for people of color, what did it mean to be "Black"? At first it meant at least one-fourth of your bloodline could be traced to a Black ancestor. If one of your grandparents was Black, you too would have that designation. In time, the parameters continued to change. Later the definition was expanded to one-eighth, then one-sixteenth, and so on until the era of slavery and the Jim Crow South (more on that later) when the "one-drop rule" was established. During that time, a single drop of "Black blood" defined someone as "Black."[3] By then, "race" had nothing to do with biology and had everything to do with how we saw ourselves socially to separate ourselves from one another.

An equally confusing question was, "What does it mean to be 'white'?" How do you classify Native Americans? Australian aborigines? Eastern Indians? At the time, the Irish were not even considered to be white. In his book, *How the Irish Became White*, author

---

3   F. James Davis, "Who Is Black? One Nation's Definition," *Frontline*, https://www.pbs.org/wgbh/pages/frontline/shows/jefferson/mixed/onedrop.html.

Noel Ignatiev opens his Introduction with exactly the point we are examining here:

> No biologist has ever been able to provide a satisfactory definition of "race"—that is, a definition that includes all members of a given race and excludes all others. Attempts to give the term a biological foundation lead to absurdities: parents and children of different races, or the well-known phenomenon that a white woman can give birth to a black child, but a black woman can never give birth to a white child. The only logical conclusion is that people are members of different races because they have been assigned to them.[4]

The daughters in this family are fraternal twins. They were born from the same womb at the same time, yet their physical characteristics are markedly different.

It is not skin color or physical characteristics that make us who we are. Above are photos of parents who by all appearances seem very much alike in terms of what some people would call race, along with their twin daughters. The children are pictured at a very young age, and again as teenagers. They are fraternal twins, born from the same womb at the same time, yet one has white skin and blue eyes while the other has dark skin and brown eyes. Anyone would classify one as "white," and the other as "Black," but there is clearly no significant biological difference.

The Human Race Machine, a public art project designed by Nancy Burson, is a computerized device that, with the click of a digital camera, allows people to see what they would look like with the facial features

4   Noel Ignatiev, *How the Irish Became White* (New York: Routledge, 1995), p. 1.

and skin-color gradations of six different nationalities. When studies were done to see how participants reacted to these "different people," the researchers got some surprising responses. They asked which one would be the most trustworthy . . . which had higher integrity . . . which was the least reliable. The vastly different responses among people of different races reflected less of what they literally saw and more about what they had been taught about people of other colors. Many of our opinions about race appear to be much more deeply rooted in inherited prejudices rather than what we see with our own eyes. All of us, with the rare exception of albinos, have melanin in our system. The level of melanin determines our skin color, ranging from very, very light to very, very dark.

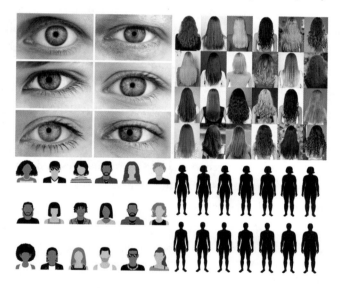

EIGHT BILLION SIBLINGS

Despite those variations in skin color, along with a few other minor physical differences, human beings are much more alike than any other species on earth. The National Human Genome Research Institute has determined that the genetic similarity between one human and any other human is 99.9 percent. That means the person sitting next to you is 99.9 percent exactly like you. That percentage is not affected by the gender of the person, the color of her skin, or the country he is from.

In fact, in many ways, genetics makes a mockery of race. The characteristics of normal human variation we use to determine broad social categories of race—such as Black, Asian, or white—are mostly things like skin color, morphological features, or hair texture, and those are all biologically encoded.

But when we look at the full genomes from people all over the world, those differences represent a tiny fraction of the differences between people. There is, for instance, more genetic diversity *within* Africa than in the rest of the world put together. If you take someone from Ethiopia and someone from the Sudan, they are more likely to be *more* genetically different from each other than either one of those people is to anyone else on the planet![5]

Do you know how powerful that is? There are no trees, no flowers, no plants, no fish, and not even apes that are as genetically alike as human beings. I want to make it clear: I am not a scientist, but what little I can understand about the science of genetics is fascinating. All the scientific talk about genomes, DNA, chromosomes, and such can get confusing to us pastors and other non-scientists, but here is one explanation that has helped me:

> A genome is all of a living thing's genetic material. It is the entire set of hereditary instructions for building, running, and maintaining an organism, and passing life on to the next generation. The whole shebang.
>
> In most living things, the genome is made of a chemical called DNA. The genome contains genes, which are packaged in chromosomes and affect specific characteristics of the organism.

---

5   Simon Worrall, quoting British geneticist Adam Rutherford in "Why Race Is Not a Thing, According to Genetics," *National Geographic*, Oct. 14, 2017, https://www.nationalgeographic.com/news/2017/10/genetics-history-race-neanderthal-rutherford/.

Imagine these relationships as a set of Chinese boxes nested one inside the other. The largest box represents the genome. Inside it, a smaller box represents the chromosomes. Inside that is a box representing genes, and inside that, finally, is the smallest box, the DNA. . . .

Each one of earth's species has its own distinctive genome: the dog genome, the wheat genome, the genomes of the cow, cold virus, bok choy, *Escherichia coli* (a bacterium that lives in the human gut and in animal intestines), and so on.

So genomes belong to species, but they also belong to individuals. . . . Unless you are an identical twin, your genome is different from that of every other person on earth—in fact, it is different from that of every other person who has ever lived.[6]

The more closely related two people are, the more similar their genomes. If you compared your genome to anyone else's, you would discover (if you bothered to count) more than three million differences. Yet we have seen that we are all 99.9 percent the same in regard to our DNA. Here is another way of looking at that:

If the genome were a book, every person's book would contain the same paragraphs and chapters, arranged in the same order. Each book would tell more or less the same story. But my book might contain a typo on page 303 that yours lacks, and your book might use a British spelling on page 135—"colour"—where mine uses the American spelling—"color."[7]

It can boggle the mind to consider that you are 99.9 percent exactly like every other human on the planet (current population: 7.8 billion). Because I am approaching this topic of race from the perspective of a pastor and an African American, I get very excited about these discoveries. They just scream to me about who God is. I do not know how all those highly intelligent scientists are interpreting their findings, but to me, it confirms that there really was an Adam and an Eve.

---

6   Sarah E. DeWeerdt, "What's a Genome?" *Genome News Network*, Jan. 15, 2003, http://www.genomenewsnetwork.org/resources/whats_a_genome/Chp1_1_1.shtml#genome1.

7   Sarah E. DeWeerdt, "Genome Variations," *Genome News Network*, Jan. 15, 2003, http://www.genomenewsnetwork.org/resources/whats_a_genome/Chp4_1.shtml.

The Bible tells us that God not only created us, but also created us in His image (Genesis 1:27). I have always believed that to be true. I have taken it on faith that I was made in the likeness of God, as was everyone else. Now, as geneticists are beginning to describe precisely how alike we are as human beings, it seems they are catching up with what God proclaimed a long time ago. Beneath all the skin colors, all the physical distinctions, all the different cultures in the world, we need to begin to see one another more as God sees us: alike . . . the same . . . equal.

Therefore, because people of all colors are so amazingly similar, we should realize how harmful it is to oppress, discriminate against, or show prejudice toward others. We will spend a lot of time discussing those issues in future chapters.

Why are we still off-base about race? One reason is that people make judgments on what they can see, and what we see does not provide all the facts. Science verifies that despite our varying skin colors and other physical traits, all humans are essentially alike. Yet those visible differences in skin color have been sufficient to cause us to make distinctions between "races," and from those distinctions has come division. We will learn more about that from sociology.

2

Shattering the Myth
of Race (Sociology)

Now that we have had a short biology lesson, you are probably left with some questions. Biology did not answer the big question for us: "What is race?" Biologically, all the "races" we define are almost exactly alike under the skin. So that leads to the next question: If people are 99.9 percent alike, why do we look so different?

PHENOTYPES

The answer, in a word, is *phenotypes*. A *phenotype* "is what you can observe about physical properties of an organism." DNA contains genes that determine certain physical traits, but those traits can vary because of different environments. Your phenotypes are determined by both your inherited genetic qualities and your environments. In the animal world, phenotypes explain why flamingos are pink—they are born white, but their diet gives them their distinctive pink color. Phenotypes demonstrate how animals in the same family can look so different sometimes, such as the different shadings of Labrador retrievers, the varying lengths of bird wings within a species, and other slight variations throughout nature.

Among humans, prominent phenotypes include eye color, hair quality, skin tone, and body shape. All eyes are alike in terms of function, composition, location in the body, and interrelation with other body parts. In other words, they all *see* alike, but they do not necessarily *look* alike. Most are either blue or brown, and some have other shades due to genetic combinations.

Sometimes physical variations are established over long periods of time. Peoples who live in sunbaked, hot climates have more exposure to UV light which causes the darkening of existing melanin, giving them a darker color for better protection from the sun than those in the Arctic north who do not need it.[8] Other times, personal choices can make a significant difference in a phenotype in a short period of time. You can inherit a genetic disposition to have a thin body shape and excellent health, but if your diet is nothing but fatty foods and you never exercise, your environment will overrule your genetics and you will round out that once-trim figure. You cannot change your genes, and you cannot always do much about your environment, but you always have a say about your personal choices.

(Since phenotypes are defined as *observable* physical properties, they also now include characteristics like levels of hormones or blood cells that can be measured in a lab.)[9]

ATTEMPTS TO CLASSIFY RACE

Stephen Jay Gould was a noted paleontologist and one of the most influential evolutionary biologists of the twentieth century. He opened an article about race with an interesting question: "Why should the most common racial group of the Western world be named for a mountain range that straddles Russia and Georgia?"

Have you ever wondered why white people are called "Caucasians"? The name originated with another noted scientist who lived two centuries before Gould, a German anatomist and naturalist named Johann

---

8   Molly Campbell, "Genotype vs. Phenotype: Examples and Definitions," *Genomics Research from Technology Networks*, Apr. 18, 2019, https://www.technologynetworks.com/genomics/ articles/genotype-vs-phenotype-examples-and-definitions-318446.

9   "phenotype / phenotypes," *Scitable* by Nature Education, https://www.nature.com/scitable/ definition/phenotype-phenotypes-35/.

Friedrich Blumenbach. His 1795 dissertation—*On the Unity of Mankind*—is considered the starting point of anthropology. Blumenbach was one of the Enlightenment's most honored scientists although his work has resulted in centuries of racial strife. He had been following the work of Carolus Linnaeus, the Swedish scientist and "father of modern taxonomy" credited with creating the first systematic method of defining and naming plants and animals. Linnaeus had categorized humans into four main categories, largely based on geographic location:

> In this work [*Systema Natura* (1758)], Linnaeus followed both continental geography and a color scheme that divided man into white European, dark Asiatic, red American, and black Negro. In the style of the times, many of the "characters" used by Linnaeus to classify his races were quite subjective and unscientific, such as "hopeful" Europeans, "sad and rigid" Asiatics, "irascible" American natives, and "calm and lazy" Africans.[10]

It appears clear from his short descriptions that Linnaeus believed, as many did at the time, in the superiority of the European peoples over others. Yet it was also clear that his classifications were based as much on geography as anything else. His official listing began with Native Americans. If he had been trying to establish a hierarchy, he surely would have started with Europeans.

Blumenbach had been following Linnaeus's work closely, and he, too, started with a four-part division of humans. That is when he chose the name "Caucasian" to describe the white Europeans, and it was not for objective scientific reasons. According to Stephen Gould's article, "Blumenbach's definition cites two reasons for his choice—the maximal beauty of people from this small region, and the probability that humans were first created in this area."

It was because Blumenbach was so enamored with the beauty of the people who lived in the Caucasus mountains that he gave

10   Kenneth E. Barber, "Johann Blumenbach and the Classification of Human Races," Encyclopedia.com, Dec. 7, 2020, https://www.encyclopedia.com/science/encyclopedias-almanacs-transcripts-and-maps/johann-blumenbach-and-classification-human-races.

light-skinned people the title of "Caucasian." However, as Blumenbach continued to revise his work, he added a fifth category to his final version in 1795, with the following results:

» The Caucasian variety, for the light-skinned people of Europe and adjacent parts of Asia and Africa;

» The Mongolian variety, for most other inhabitants of Asia, including China and Japan;

» The Ethiopian variety, for the dark-skinned people of Africa;

» The American variety, for most native populations of the New World; and

» The Malay variety, for the Polynesians and Melanesians of the Pacific and for the aborigines of Australia.

This is where the race issue comes into play. Gould explains:

This change seems so minor. Why, then, do we credit Blumenbach, rather than Linnaeus, as the founder of racial classification? (One might prefer to say "discredit," as the enterprise does not, for good reason, enjoy high repute these days.) But Blumenbach's apparently small change actually records a theoretical shift that could not have been broader, or more portentous, in scope. . . .

By moving from the Linnaean four-race system to his own five-race scheme, Blumenbach radically changed the geometry of human order from a geographically based model without explicit ranking to a hierarchy of worth, oddly based upon perceived beauty, and fanning out in two directions from a Caucasian ideal. The addition of a Malay category was crucial to this geometric reformulation. . . .

The shift from a geographic to a hierarchical ordering of human diversity must stand as one of the most fateful transitions in the history of Western science—for what, short of railroads and nuclear bombs, has had more practical impact, in this case almost entirely negative, upon our collective lives? Ironically, Blumenbach is the focus of this shift, for his five-race scheme became canonical and changed the geometry of human order from Linnaean cartography to linear ranking—in short, to a system based on putative worth.

I say ironic because Blumenbach was the least racist and most genial of all Enlightenment thinkers. How peculiar that the man most committed to human unity, and to inconsequential moral and intellectual differences among groups, should have changed the mental geometry of human order to a scheme that has served racism ever since.[11]

Multiple sources confirm that Blumenbach could hardly be accused of racism. He was among the more enlightened people of his day. He specifically refuted the claim that Africans bore physical features of inferiority: "There is no single character so peculiar and so universal among the Ethiopians, but what it may be observed on the one hand everywhere in other varieties of men."

Changes in skin color, he said, could occur over many generations, whether lighter to darker, or darker to lighter: "Color, whatever be its cause, be it bile, or the influence of the sun, the air, or the climate, is, at all events, an adventitious and easily changeable thing, and can never constitute a diversity of species." Blumenbach defended the mental and moral unity of all peoples and had exceptionally strong beliefs that black Africans and white Europeans had equal status. A special library in his home was comprised exclusively of works by Black authors. Yet because Blumenbach's model was a hierarchy and was based on the rather subjective evaluation of certain European people as being "the most beautiful race of men," his work was used by subsequent generations to justify racism.[12]

"Race" was a term that had been in occasional use since probably the 1400s, but it gained a more widespread and focused usage after the work of Linnaeus and Blumenbach. Johann Blumenbach could never have anticipated what would be the long-term results of his work. It certainly was not something he would have endorsed:

Gradually it became obvious that human variation was based not on different genes, but rather on varying frequencies of the same genes shared by all populations of humans. No classification system that

---

11 Stephen Jay Gould, "The Geometer of Race," *Discover*, Nov. 1, 1994, https://www. discovermagazine.com/mind/the-geometer-of-race.

12 Ibid.

separated humans into distinct species, or even sub-species could hold up under the light of these sciences.

Still, by the end of the nineteenth century, the idea of a hierarchy of races that elevated some nations and people above others, was widely accepted by many in the upper classes of Europe, Great Britain, and the United States. The wealthy and powerful were often smug in the belief that their superior station and position was justified and secured by nature. Theological dogma was interwoven into this debate and many attempts were made to sort the various races into a pattern purportedly designed by the Creator.

In this way, races were incorrectly seen as preordained, pure, and rigidly fixed in their current form. This erroneous belief has survived into the present despite the advances of evolution, genetics, and psychology.[13]

Another writer, Raj Bhopal, concludes:

Blumenbach's work was a turning point in the history of race and science, although it was nearly 200 years before the lessons were properly absorbed. Blumenbach's legacy is tarnished by biases and errors, and it teaches us that even great scientists can be led astray by personal views (such as notions about beauty) shaped by the ethos of their times. . . . Blumenbach's name has been associated with scientific racism, but his arguments actually undermined racism. Blumenbach could not have foreseen the coming abuse of his ideas and classification in the 19th and (first half of the) 20th centuries.

We continue to struggle with the complexity of the concepts of race and ethnicity, and the resultant imperfect classifications, in our multiethnic world. Now, Blumenbach's varieties of humanity can be seen in virtually every major city, and through the visual media, globally. Blumenbach's thinking, despite its faults, continues to be relevant, inspiring, and illuminating.[14]

---

13 Barber, "Johann Blumenbach . . ."

14 Raj Bhopal, "The Beautiful Skull and Blumenbach's Errors: The Birth of the Scientific Concept of Race," *BMJ*, Dec. 22, 2007, https://www.ncbi.nlm.nih.gov/pmc/articles/PMC2151154/.

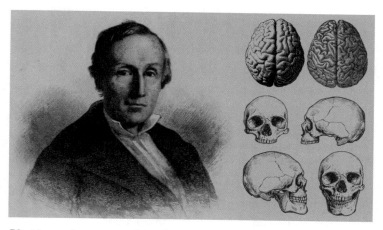

*Physician and anatomy professor Samuel Morton believed he could measure peo-
ple's intellectual capacities by measuring and comparing the sizes of their crania.*

Samuel Morton, shown in the above illustration, was an American
doctor who lived during the first half of the nineteenth century. He
didn't believe the biblical creation story, and he set out to prove his
hypothesis that human beings were comprised of different species,
not varieties of the same species. He thought he could differentiate
those different species by measuring their intellectual capabilities,
and the way he tried to prove it was by measuring and comparing
cranial size. He began to collect skulls from the five groups he had
identified: Ethiopian (African), Native American, Caucasian, Malay,
and Mongolian, eventually assembling 900 or so. He literally measured the circumference of their crania to find out how large they
were, but he had begun with the preconceived opinion that Caucasians had larger heads than the rest. And he made the false assump-
tion that larger heads meant larger brains and therefore, more
intelligence. (He made no consideration of body size, which is a
better indicator. People with bigger bodies have bigger brains.)

Morton used pepper seeds and, later, lead shot to fill the skulls
and see which held the most. His conclusion was that Caucasians

had the largest skull size and Africans had the smallest. Most people who study his work believe his measurements were fastidious and well-intentioned. But as one noted, "Just because Morton's data were not biased doesn't mean his science wasn't. He can measure skulls very accurately but also be a biased scientist." The racial categories he had determined had no biological basis. Consequently, Morton is remembered as largely responsible for "scientific racism," and his work was cited long thereafter to justify slavery.[15]

Let me tell you how impactful Morton's study was. In the mid-1800s as debates raged between abolitionists and pro-slavery factions, the government was trying to keep a balance between free states and slave states. (More details in later chapters.) Texas was applying for statehood and wanted to be a slave state, which the abolitionists were opposing. With Abraham Lincoln coming into the presidency, there was concern that he would side with the abolitionists. Therefore, when the official decision was being made, Dr. Morton's biased, incorrect, unscientific material was used as "proof" that the less intelligent Blacks needed the aid of whites to watch over them. The pro-slavery faction won the case, and Texas was brought in as a slave state. When it was, it essentially began the countdown to the Civil War.

In subsequent tests, every part of a Black man has been examined and measured—the Black man's hand, the Black man's foot, the Black man's head. Why? Because there was a constant search to find scientific evidence that Blacks were different from (inferior to) white-skinned people. Let me tell you something. During all those searches, they never found a difference. And in some cases when they could not find the results they were looking for, people actually lied about the data. They wanted scientific proof for different "races," but science cannot prove something that is not true.

---

15   Paul Wolff Mitchell and Janet Monge, "A New Take on the 19th-century Skull Collection of Samuel Morton," *Science Daily*, Oct. 4, 2018, https://www.sciencedaily.com/releases/2018/10/181004143943.htm.

SHATTERING THE MYTH OF RACE

So, we have seen that people see different skin colors and point to biology as a determiner of "race," yet biology insists that all human beings are 99.9 percent alike. It also alerts us to phenotypes that, although they create clearly observable distinctions in such physical traits as skin color and eye color, have only slight cosmetic differences—inconsequential in terms of making one group of people any better or worse than another. Yet even after science disproves any validity about the superiority of one group over another (particularly regarding skin color), that concept lives on because many in society *choose* to differentiate between groups of people based on such surface standards. The conflicts around race are not rooted in the truths of science. Race is not a matter of biology; it is a tragic consequence of misguided sociology.

Most of us have some combination of theology (religious beliefs based on personal experience and investigation) and sociology (what we have been taught, observations, prejudgments, and best efforts to figure things out). To arrive at a helpful and healthful understanding of race, we need to ensure that our theology comes first and our sociology—the way we see the world—follows. Too many people in the world have so far allowed their sociology to inform their theology. They have created a sociology that became almost divine. Sociology should not determine who we are. Who we really are, are the children of God. Certainly, I celebrate being an African American. I am proud of my cultural distinctions. But first, I belong to the body of Christ, and then I am brothers with whoever else belongs to the body of Christ. This understanding must supersede my ethnicity.

Yet much of the nation during the eighteenth and nineteenth centuries put sociology above theology and (mis)used the work of Linnaeus and Blumenbach to establish a hierarchy of races where dark-skinned people were deemed to be of lower status than white people.

Another reason "race" became such a critical issue during the nineteenth century was, frankly, greed. America was fast becoming one of the most powerful nations on the planet, and one of its greatest assets was cotton. In addition, America offered to the world tobacco, sugar, and other goods that were planted, raised, and harvested with slave labor. Slavery was driving the economy. Landowners and investors who were becoming overwhelmingly rich from free labor did not question the rightness or wrongness of slavery.

African Americans were not the only labor force. Indentured servants from various places in Europe also agreed to serve until their debts were paid, but if they were mistreated and abused, they could run away and blend in with the residents of some nearby city. But African Americans were easily identifiable if they tried to escape, and they had no way to return to their homelands. As you will see as we go through this book, once society wrongly accepted the subjugation of dark-skinned peoples, attempts to resolve that egregious offense have lasted until this day. Future chapters will provide many examples throughout history of the atrocities that arose from the simplistic, unscientific, and unrighteous ways culture began to *think* about race.

Our world has developed so that today we see race everywhere we look. Can you sit down and talk about politics and not talk about race? No. Can you talk about history and not talk about race? No. Can you talk about psychology, or even sociology, and not talk about race? No. In fact, we often lead with the "race" discussion instead of addressing a widespread national issue. Rather than saying, "Here's a fifth generation of people who are living in a culture of poverty, which helps to explain why they behave the way they behave," we attribute the problem to race. I do not believe sociology should ever be taught by race categories because it infers that there is something biologically different in different people. True, the *cultural* distinctions are very significant, but we will never arrive at satisfying answers by saying that the problem is race because, very simply, it is not.

Going hand in hand with the issue of racial categorization is the ongoing problem of oppression. The separation of people by skin color always leads to oppression of one group by the other. Those in power stop the others from getting ahead by intentionally placing a ceiling that prevents them from getting an advantage. When power reinforces oppression, the result is *discrimination*. Rather than people being encouraged (or even allowed) to do their best, they are met with illogical and unreasonable limits. The result does not help anyone.

I will provide many examples throughout this book, but let me start with this one. During World War II, racial discrimination was still a very real problem. African Americans were just as eager to serve their country as anyone, yet when they enlisted, they were often assigned menial jobs while white soldiers did the "important" work. Black men who wanted to be pilots were usually denied because it was believed (without proof) that they did not have the intelligence to fly a plane. It was also speculated that the arteries in their blood vessels were too small and the G-forces would cause them to pass out during flights.

In 1939, the government began to sponsor flight schools at a variety of colleges, but when they would not do so at Black colleges, a student at Howard University filed a lawsuit. He soon had support from the NAACP, Black newspapers, and even Franklin and Eleanor Roosevelt. The result was the "Tuskegee Experiment." A flight school was initiated at Tuskegee University in Alabama. In July of 1941, the Army Air Corps (a precursor of the Air Force) began a program with twelve cadets and one officer, all African Americans. Most people expected this "experiment" to fail, but these and subsequent pilots became known as the Tuskegee Airmen and quickly gained a well-deserved reputation for courage and success as they flew combat missions in Italy and escorted bombers.

Nine hundred twenty-six Black servicemen graduated from Tuskegee during an era when racist attitudes were officially sanctioned in the military. Tuskegee pilots earned some of the most impressive military records in history, and in doing so, shamed the American military into fully integrating in 1948, advancing the civil rights movement. Captain Benjamin O. Davis Jr., the officer over the first twelve cadets, later became the first African American general in the Air Force.[16]

The Tuskegee Airmen never lost one bomber that they flew to protect. They proved that it was not really a lack of skill or ability that kept Black people from flying planes. The problem was not incompetence; it was discrimination and oppression that prevented qualified people from advancing.

For further insight into this issue, I recommend you watch the movie *Black Wings*. The movie explains that most of the Blacks who were eventually chosen for the Tuskegee Airmen were already pilots. The question was not really, "Can a Black person fly a plane?" It was, "Do we really want to see Black pilots in our military?"

At about the same time, another example arose from the world of sports. Germany was hosting the 1936 Olympic Games in Berlin, and had the most participants—348, all of whom conformed to Germany's Aryans-only policy. Several world-class athletes who happened to be Jewish, Gypsy, or people of color were not allowed to participate for Germany.

The United States attended the competition with 312 athletes that included five Jews and nineteen African Americans. The Olympics had been established to promote goodwill among all nations by demonstrating racial equality in sporting competition, but the Nazis, of course, did not believe in the equality of races. Their purpose was to highlight their Aryan athletes, believing them to be naturally superior based purely on race.

Germany did emerge as the victor with a total of eighty-nine medals. The United States came in second, with fifty-six medals.[17]

---

16   Melissa T. Miller, "The Tuskegee Airmen," Military.com, https://www.military.com/history/the-tuskegee-airmen.html.

17   "The Berlin Olympics," *The History Place*, Accessed Dec. 3, 2020, https://www.historyplace.com/worldwar2/triumph/tr-olympics.html.

But the talk of the games was America's Jesse Owens, who quickly shattered the myth of Aryan superiority by emerging as the most successful individual athlete at the games, winning gold medals in the 100-meter dash, 200-meter dash, long jump, and 4 x 100 relay. These Olympic victories and many other sports feats and records came more than a decade before Jackie Robinson broke the race barrier and began to play baseball in the previously all-white leagues.

Yet even decades later, it was difficult for African Americans to be perceived as equals in all aspects of sports. In the early years of professional football, it was quite rare to see a Black quarterback. The quarterbacks were the thinkers . . . the leaders . . . the face of the team. It took many years for fans to become comfortable seeing African Americans in that key position.

HOW RACISM CREEPS INTO CULTURE

Many times the law has been used to legislate discrimination. In fact, sometimes racism becomes more evident when laws are enacted. Monkeys currently are not able to drive cars, so you do not see any laws prohibiting it. But as soon as monkeys prove they can drive, then the powerful will desire to oppress them. Therefore, they must pass laws to do so. Laws are passed only when the ability exists. When Blacks began to see laws passed prohibiting them from attending certain schools or living in certain neighborhoods, they knew it was not because they were incapable of getting degrees or paying off their mortgages. If that were the case, the law would have been unnecessary. They saw such laws for what they were—clear signs of prejudice and discrimination that kept them from moving toward greater equality in our nation.

In the past, the legal system has actually legitimized race. Laws were passed with racism written right into them. It became against the law for Blacks to marry whites. They could not sit just anywhere on a bus or train. They could not hold certain jobs or live in certain locations. Race does not exist, biologically, yet we have used race to establish all these hurtful and unfair distinctions between groups of people who are almost exactly alike.

Just as civil laws have tended to divide the races on many occasions, the media often adds fuel to the fire. You might remember the Blaxploitation films of the 1970s: *Shaft, Superfly, Cleopatra Jones, Blacula,* and others. They elevated many Black actors from minor roles and sidekicks to leading characters, yet they were frequently criticized for portraying those characters in stereotypical, one-dimensional ways. Most films in this genre were marked by violence, drug use, and sexual activity to play to a ready audience. A disparaging image of Black people spread not just in the United States but all over the world.

Media also tends to use labels for people and groups. When you hear the term "street gang," what image comes to your mind? Most people will think of a mean-looking group of Blacks or Latinos because we hear so much about "Black gangs" or "Latino gangs." You do not hear so much, however, about "white gangs." Do you think there are no white gangs out there? Instead, the newscasts speak of "organized crime" or use some other label. But if you are referring to a group of thugs who carry unlicensed weapons, deal drugs, occasionally shoot and kill people, and then share the money they get from it all, you are describing a gang, whatever else you choose to call it.

Race-related language can be subtle. If you refer to someone as being "fair-skinned," it is usually taken as a compliment. Why? Did you intentionally intend to infer that the whiter someone is, the better? Not likely. Yet how is a beautiful young Black child supposed to feel when she hears such a compliment directed to someone else? "Fair-skinned" suggests a color scale where lighter is positive, so where does that leave darker?

In contrast, let us consider the word "black," attempting to leave racial issues aside for a moment. Think of the connotations when you hear phrases like *black cats, black magic,* or *black ops.* When "black" is used as an adjective, the word is tinged with a sense of secrecy, danger, or even evil. So when the same word is used to describe a person, don't you suspect those subtle associations might sometimes influence our perceptions?

We need to evaluate how we have been trained to think and speak in ways that can be unintentionally insensitive or harmful to others. Perhaps you think I am nitpicking a bit here. These seem like such inconsequential offenses. Yet as we continue our examination of race, we will see how racial inequality can gradually infiltrate all our interactions and institutions to the point where people do not realize just how discriminatory they are. At that point, racism becomes *systemic*. When schools accept only certain races, and then companies only hire from those schools, and then city leaders and officials arise from those companies, the system has already prequalified who will succeed and who will fail. People sometimes point to bad neighborhoods and point out that they are Black neighborhoods, which might be true, but they rarely see the systemic racial discrimination that created the problem to begin with. We need to understand how such systemic problems arise and how they affect the whole fabric of our society.

If systemic racism goes unchecked, it can become *structural* racism. Groups who hate or fear other races can literally construct the world around them to promote racism. When people of like (but corrupt) thinking are spread out through various levels of the legal system, they can begin to influence who gets arrested by the police, who resides over the trials, how suspects are treated in jail, and so forth. After such a structure is established, racism continues to flourish throughout the system.

Structural racism is worse than just a few people "falling through the cracks in the system." In recent years, it has been startling to see how many Black males would have died on death row, falsely accused of murder, until DNA evidence proved they could not have committed the crime for which they were accused. When witnesses came forward with false accusations (whether erroneously or intentionally), the system was in place to structurally hold them, position them, and keep them in their place. Thanks to the Innocence Project[18], many such falsely accused people are being freed, although some have already spent decades in prison.

I want to assure you that God is aware of all who have been denied their rights. God's presence is still very much with people who fight for justice. But the more of us who inform ourselves of such problems and choose to get involved, the sooner we will begin to see positive results.

Why are we still off-base about race? One primary reason is that "race" should not even exist. The concept was initiated centuries ago after an erroneous classification of human beings, and the damaging consequences of that mistake have persisted ever since. Minorities continue to struggle because of severe social inequalities that often create widespread pain and suffering.

---

18 See https://innocenceproject.org/.

3

Prejudice, Racism, and Hate (Anthropology)

In 1967, when I was in the third grade, my family moved into a white neighborhood in Chicago. We were not welcomed with open arms, and in fact, we were not welcomed at all. It was not long before "white flight" began. Before they left, many whites expressed their extreme displeasure at our presence in their neighborhood. My brother was beaten up, and we were sometimes chased home from school by kids wielding chains and bats. We learned to run like the wind!

One day on my way home after school, a student walked up to me, called me the "n word," and stabbed me in the thigh with a geometric compass. Those things are sharp! As I writhed in pain, I was also disturbed and confused. What would cause an older student to be so angry that he would attack a little Black boy? It had to be he was taught that Black was so offensive he had to lash out against it.

That was a very difficult year for me. The stares, nasty words, and physical threats caused me to wonder if there was something so very wrong with me that it was right for people to treat me with such contempt. My parents told me again and again that I am a person of infinite worth, created in the image of God. My blackness is not a flaw; it is just part of God's design for me. Finally, I realized it was not my fault that other people acted that way. It was their problem, not mine.

INTRO TO ANTHROPOLOGY

Anthropology is defined as "the science that deals with your origins, physical and cultural development, biological characteristics, and social customs and beliefs." In this chapter, I would like to convince you to expand your interpretation of that definition. It is helpful to be aware of your human anthropological roots, of course, but let's not stop there.

It is beautiful if you want to celebrate being of European descent, an African American, a Native American, Hispanic, Asian, or whatever your ancestry happens to be. It is an acknowledgment of thanksgiving for who God created you to be. But God forbid that we ever celebrate those ethnicities more than we celebrate what it means to be part of the family of God. After we look *backward* and celebrate where we came from, then let us start looking *outward* to spread the gospel of Jesus Christ among every ethnicity—the only solution that can make all people one again. As we strive to resolve racial tensions in our world, let us also keep in mind our spiritual origins, our ongoing spiritual development, our Christian behavior, and our beliefs.

God made only one race of people. He gathered us together in Him. And when we operate and move in His anointing and what He has called us to do, we are His called-out ones. Our mission is to pray, to proclaim the power of the Almighty God to the world, and to bring about healing, wisdom, knowledge, and miracles in the earth.

In our initial look at the issue of race so far, we have already seen that much of what is defined or described as "race" is really a myth. We need to challenge more of what we have been told and taught—to either verify it as truth or expose it as a lie. Certainly, these days we need to question anything we see or hear on television and social media. But we also would be wise to reconsider things we were taught as children and even the "truths" that are passed along to us from friends and family members.

Ultimately, I hope we will learn to get our news feeds from heaven instead of this world. We must not be so trusting of everything our sociology tells us. We need to be more trusting of the things our loving God teaches through His Word. When we do, we can begin to celebrate our diversity and our differences. But we celebrate *cultural* distinctions, not biological separations.

Culture shapes who we become more than we might realize. If you travel the world and observe the vast differences in cultures, you might begin to question the biological truth that we are all 99.9 percent alike. Yet if you adopt a newborn from Asia and bring him home to Texas, he will sound like a Texan when he begins to speak. As babies babble while they are learning to talk, they mimic the sounds they are hearing. The words—and the accents—are derived from the culture in which the child is raised. They are not prewired in the baby.

Many of the opinions and beliefs that we hold so deeply are only cultural influences. Are there differences between the cultures? Oh, yes, there are. Because people grow up in geographically different locations, we have different languages, customs, religions, and ancestry, but those differences do not change the fact that we are biologically the same exact people.

Just because we come from different parts of the world and speak different languages does not mean that God did not create all of us from Adam and Eve. It does not mean that some of us were created in His image and others of us were not. You may be Asian, East Indian, African, Native American, Latino, European, Inuit, Australian aborigine, or some other cultural distinction, but you were created in the image of God just like everyone else.

We need to keep that in mind as we continue our examination of race because we are about to see how some people throughout history have keyed in on those cultural differences and somehow created the myth of race—that certain groups are superior to other groups. Some people even insist that God created us that way. Do not believe that message for a moment.

PREJUDICE AND/OR DISCRIMINATION

Prejudice and discrimination are problems among most all cultures and ethnicities. But here in America, have you ever wondered why the issues almost always seem more intense between whites and Blacks?

By the time the Europeans began to settle in the American colonies in the early 1600s, they had discovered many ethnicities already here. They immediately began to encounter tribes of Native Americans, and as they moved progressively west, they discovered more and more native tribes. Many historians speculate that they originated in Asia and eventually migrated through what is now Russia, across the Bering Strait into Canada, and then spread throughout North and South America. The friendships developed between the first Pilgrims and the natives who helped them learn to survive marked a hopeful beginning, but it was not to last. When Native American settlements began to impede European expansion, the overwhelmingly outnumbered natives were victims of broken treaties, forcible removal, and worse.

French and Spanish explorers had been active for well over a century and had begun to claim land for their respective countries. In time, clashes would arise between various European nations on American soil.

African Americans also began to arrive . . . but they all came on slave ships. As other peoples continued to flock to the New World in search of adventure, opportunity, wealth, and other goals, those from Africa came in subjugation. They had no choice of coming and no other options when they arrived. From the time they set foot on the shores of America, they were enslaved. The next chapter will provide more details of their initial arrival in 1619. It would take two and a half centuries before they would be free of slavery, and then they were still a long way from equality. After another century and a half, they are still working toward that goal. Slavery has been outlawed, but prejudice and discrimination have been alive and well to this day.

If we want to influence our own culture for the better—to reduce the systemic racism that can infiltrate cultural thinking—we need to understand and speak the truth. As we do, we ought to start with ourselves. Do we, at times, contribute to the problem of prejudice and discrimination? Do we even know the difference?

If you are prejudiced, it means you have racist feelings and emotions toward somebody or some group of people. If you discriminate, it means you actively oppose them through your words and actions.

Robert K. Merton, who is pictured below, gave this matter a great deal of thought. He was a twentieth-century American pioneer in the field of sociology. His seventy-plus years of experience resulted in the nickname of "Mr. Sociology" and his involvement in many relevant areas of life led to the coining of numerous terms such as *self-fulfilling prophecy* and *role models*. Merton's studies on integration were used in the *Brown v. Board of Education* Supreme Court case.[19] His observations on prejudice and discrimination provide much rel-

Merton received an honorary doctorate in sociology from Leiden University, Belgium, in 1965.

evant insight as we consider issues of race. He reflected on what he called the "American creed" set forth in the Declaration of Independence, the preamble of the Constitution, and the Bill of Rights.

---

19   Michael T. Kaufman, "Robert K. Merton, Versatile Sociologist and Father of the Focus Group, Dies at 92," *New York Times*, Feb. 24, 2003, https://www.nytimes.com/2003/02/24/nyregion/robert-k-merton-versatile-sociologist-and-father-of-the-focus-group-dies-at-92.html.

The creed asserts the indefeasible principle of the human right to full equity—the right of equitable access to justice, freedom, and opportunity, irrespective of race or religion or ethnic origin. It proclaims further the universalist doctrine of the dignity of the individual, irrespective of the groups of which he is a part. It is a creed announcing full moral equities for all, not an absurd myth affirming the equality of intellectual and physical capacity of all people everywhere. And it goes on to say that although individuals differ in innate endowment, they do so as individuals, not by virtue of their group memberships.[20]

The creed seems clear, yet people can form different beliefs and attitudes about it, and then they can act on those beliefs, or not. Merton realized a person could be prejudiced or not, and could be discriminatory or not, so he separated people into four categories.

1) The Unprejudiced Non-Discriminator
Those who are neither prejudiced nor given to discrimination comprise "the strategic group that can act as the spearhead for the progressive extension of the creed into effective practice. . . . They alone can provide the positive social environment for the other types who will no longer find it expedient or rewarding to retain their prejudices of discriminatory practices." Yet these people are not always as influential as they should be. Some tend to become self-satisfied with their enlightened outlook, and never attempt to challenge others to higher standards. Merton warns: "Goodwill is not enough to modify social reality. It is only when this goodwill is harnessed to psychological and social realities that it can be used to reach cultural objectives."

2) The Unprejudiced Discriminator
Merton describes a person in this category as someone "who, despite his own freedom from prejudice, supports discriminatory practices when it is the easier or more profitable course." For example, he says, an employer may not hold any personal prejudice against Blacks or Jews, yet is aware that other people do, so he refuses to hire them. In doing so, however, most people in this category eventually suffer from varying degrees of shame and guilt.

20   Robert K. Merton, *Sociological Ambivalence and Other Essays* (New York: The Free Press, 1976), p. 190.

3) The Prejudiced Non-Discriminator

Many of us probably know someone who is obviously prejudiced, yet knows when to keep his personal beliefs to himself out of opportunity for personal gain or self-protection. Some are more open about their prejudice than others, such as employers who stop discriminating only when forced to do so by legal requirements or commands coming down from upper management. Others might willingly hide their prejudice when they find a large market among the people they would not normally associate with. And then there are the racists who spew their hate speech until they find themselves in the company of more powerful people who do not share their prejudiced beliefs.

4) The Prejudiced Discriminator

In Merton's words, this is someone who is "the bigot pure and unashamed, the man of prejudice consistent in his departures from the American creed. In some measure, he is found everywhere in the land. . . . He considers differential treatment of Negro and white not as 'discrimination,' in the sense of unfair treatment, but as 'discriminating,' in the sense of showing acute discernment."[21]

People often insist they are not racist, and by that, they mean they are not both prejudiced *and* discriminatory. Yet if they are honest, they might see themselves in the second or third of Merton's categories. Many of us deceive ourselves for years because we never really give the matter sufficient thought, or when we do, we are reluctant to admit our true feelings.

Those internal thoughts and beliefs need to be dealt with. They need to be surrendered to the power of God. The next step, then, is to conform our actions to those surrendered thoughts. What good does it do to believe everyone is equal if, the next time you get around your prejudiced friends or coworkers, you do not say anything? You might even go along with them. You do not believe other cultural groups are any different from you, yet you discriminate against them just because your friends do. That means that you are being made and molded and fashioned after your friends, not after Christ.

---

21   Ibid. pp. 189-199 or see canvas.harvard.edu › files › download.

We need to examine ourselves closely and purge prejudice wherever we find it, whether in our thoughts, our feelings, or our behavior. We can never overcome racism until we are able to think right, feel right, and act right. We need to ask God in all His power and glory to change our hearts, increase our love for others, and provide a holistic transformation from our prejudicial and discriminatory ways to a lifestyle that honors Him. I do not want to mistreat or harm anyone else who is in the image of God. I want to remember that everyone—the little ones, the "least" in society, and everybody else—deserves my honor and respect because they all reflect God's image.

SPIRITUAL ANTHROPOLOGY

Chapter 10 will focus on theology, but we need to take a short journey through Scripture at this point to see how our theology and anthropology might be connected. I have already said this, but I want to reemphasize it: There was only one Adam, and there was only one Eve. God did not make five Adams and five Eves.

All the peoples of the world have come from the same mother, Eve, and the same father, Adam (Genesis 3:20). That profound truth means that everybody in the entire world is related. If we start going back five or six generations, most of us will discover people in our family trees that are going to blow our socks off because we will begin to see just how much diversity has led to the people we are today. We are all related. We are all one family, one race—the human race. To add to the wonder of that thought, believers have discovered that God is our Father. As we respond to His love and come into the body of Christ, we accept Jesus as not only our Savior, but also our brother.

From a perspective of anthropology, God sees all humanity as one people, one race, one family. We should see one another with that same perspective, but we get thrown off by all those pesky phenotypes that make us appear to be different groups of people, even when biologically we are as alike as we can be. What happened? If we all trace back to Adam and Eve, why don't we all look alike? We did at one time.

God created one group of people, but He did not want them to remain in one place. He had told humankind to "Be fruitful and multiply and fill the earth" (Genesis 9:1). But the people had other ideas:

> Now the whole earth had one language and the same words. And as people migrated from the east, they found a plain in the land of Shinar and settled there. And they said to one another, "Come, let us make bricks, and burn them thoroughly." And they had brick for stone, and bitumen for mortar. Then they said, "Come, let us build ourselves a city and a tower with its top in the heavens, and let us make a name for ourselves, lest we be dispersed over the face of the whole earth." And the Lord came down to see the city and the tower, which the children of man had built. And the Lord said, "Behold, they are one people, and they have all one language, and this is only the beginning of what they will do. And nothing that they propose to do will now be impossible for them. Come, let us go down and there confuse their language, so that they may not understand one another's speech." So the Lord dispersed them from there over the face of all the earth, and they left off building the city. Therefore its name was called Babel, because there the Lord confused the language of all the earth. And from there the Lord dispersed them over the face of all the earth (Genesis 11:1-9).

Prior to this, God had sent the Flood to curb the sinfulness that had spread over the earth. When He wanted to break up this fresh group of defiant humans united against Him, He did not go to such extreme measures. This time He simply gave them different languages which caused them to branch off in different directions, and as they did, different cultures were created. It brought a halt to the oneness God had created, but that would be remedied later. That is right: God created one race of people with everyone just alike. Then when they rebelled against Him, He compelled them to establish different cultures by eliminating their universal method of communication, replacing it with many different languages.

It is at this point that God initiates *ethnogenesis*—the creation and development of ethnic groups. Does not that negate what He did at Creation? It may seem so, but it was a result of a fallen nature. He put Plan A on hold until the people were ready to proceed with it. That time would come on the Day of Pentecost, as the Holy Spirit arrived to empower the church to carry on the ministry Jesus Christ had begun:

> When the day of Pentecost arrived, they were all together in one place. And suddenly there came from heaven a sound like a mighty rushing wind, and it filled the entire house where they were sitting. And divided tongues as of fire appeared to them and rested on each one of them. And they were all filled with the Holy Spirit and began to speak in other tongues as the Spirit gave them utterance. Now there were dwelling in Jerusalem Jews, devout men from every nation under heaven. And at this sound the multitude came together, and they were bewildered, because each one was hearing them speak in his own language. And they were amazed and astonished, saying, "Are not all these who are speaking Galileans? And how is it that we hear, each of us in his own native language? Parthians and Medes and Elamites and residents of Mesopotamia, Judea and Cappadocia, Pontus and Asia, Phrygia and Pamphylia, Egypt and the parts of Libya belonging to Cyrene, and visitors from Rome, both Jews and proselytes, Cretans and Arabians—we hear them telling in our own tongues the mighty works of God." And all were amazed and perplexed, saying to one another, "What does this mean?" But others mocking said, "They are filled with new wine" (Acts 2:1-13).

When God used a variety of languages to break up the crowd at the Tower of Babel and send them to various parts of the earth, He already had a plan to restore a common language and unite all the cultures again. Just as it was at Creation, God's intent is still that we will all be together as one. It would be several centuries later, but the plan was already laid out. The restoration of unity would begin with the coming of Jesus, and it would continue with the formation and growth of the church, directed and empowered by the Holy Spirit.

Jesus' last recorded words on earth were a promise: "It is not for you to know times or seasons that the Father has fixed by his own authority. But you will receive power when the Holy Spirit has come upon you, and you will be my witnesses in Jerusalem and in all Judea and Samaria, and to the end of the earth" (Acts 1:7-8).

Many of those remote parts of the earth were represented in Jerusalem on the Day of Pentecost. You can count almost twenty in the passage above, and there were almost certainly many more. In fact, there were "devout men from every nation under heaven" (Acts 2:5). But rather than needing dozens of interpreters for all those people as Peter spoke about Jesus, they all heard the gospel in their own language, miraculously, by the power of God. Remember, God was the one who started new languages. And on this day, He eradicated the language barriers that separate us and began to bring all cultures back together again.

Shortly before Jesus' final promise, He had left believers with a challenge: "All authority in heaven and on earth has been given to me. Go therefore and make disciples of all nations, baptizing them in the name of the Father and of the Son and of the Holy Spirit, teaching them to observe all that I have commanded you. And behold, I am with you always, to the end of the age" (Matthew 28:18-20). Our faith in Jesus and the spiritual transformation that results makes us "a new creation" (2 Corinthians 5:17). We become the *ethnos*—a new ethnic group in Jesus comprised of believers from all the tribes and families scattered across the world. The diversity that God mandated at the Tower of Babel is replaced with eternal unity for those who belong to the family of God. On the Day of Pentecost, God gave individuals the power of the Holy Spirit, so they could begin to reunite people in the name of the Lord.

I want us to keep these things in mind as we continue to examine the issues around race. I know many conscientious and empathic people who desperately want to resolve all our racial issues immediately. Every time they see a new example of injustice—and such examples are all too common, even today—the pain they witness fuels their passion. For some, their righteous anger eventually evolves into outright rage. I urge us not to let our anger transform into violence or hatred. As we look for more effective short-term solutions to the problems that arise from racism, let us never forget that God already has the long-term solution. Unity and peace are promised to all who follow His will. Let us put our passion into being a more dedicated church that continually reaches out in love to all people, whatever their previous shortcomings, whatever their ancestry, and whatever their skin color.

In this world of ours, we have walked on the moon, landed spacecraft on Mars, and sent probes to distant locations in our galaxy. We understand fusion and fission to the point where we can split atoms. We have accumulated so much knowledge, and yet when it comes to issues of race, we display so little wisdom. We think we know so much, yet we cannot even get along. It is time for the church to step up and become the united body of Christ so that we can honor the image of God and bring glory to His name. It is time for us to demonstrate what it means to be salt and light, so the world will look at us and think, *Wow, those people have something we don't have!* The church needs to unite and begin to lead in resolving these troubling racial divisions.

We must pay more attention to our spiritual anthropology these days—especially our customs and beliefs. At this writing, most churches are still being urged to practice social distancing if they choose to meet in person at all. But in times past, I wonder if the church has not become a bit too comfortable with distancing. We have attributed cultural differences to explain why Blacks and whites have worshiped separately for so long. "They worship differently." "They like to stand at closer proximity, and be more demonstrative than we do." "They are too solemn and quiet when we like to praise God out loud."

I understand that we all have different comfort zones, but that is no reason to excuse ourselves from ever mingling with believers of other ethnicities. I still remember how left out and unwanted I felt in my new neighborhood when I was in third grade. I never want anyone to feel that way around me. As a leader of a church, and as an individual, I want to always be welcoming to people of all other ethnicities. I want to see them as part of my family—the family that God has established. Won't you join me?

Why are we still off-base about race? As we cluster with others of our own ethnicity, we sometimes create comfort zones that can make us reluctant to step out and see how others view the world, or even to invite others into our circle. If we truly believe that God's family includes all ethnicities, we will make a point not to be so exclusive.

4

Where We Went Wrong
(History: 1619–1854)

Entire encyclopedias could be compiled and still not cover a small percentage of the history of Black people in America. It is futile to think we can go into much depth in only a few chapters, but we can touch on many of the high points and come to some understanding of how racial issues continue to plague America today.

ALWAYS ENSLAVED

Did you know that America had slaves before we had Pilgrims?

If you were paying attention in the previous chapter, you saw that the first Black people in the Americas arrived before the *Mayflower* as slaves. The date was August 20, 1619. The *Mayflower* would not land until more than a year later, on December 21, 1620. It would be almost two centuries before people of African descent on American soil would have any degree of freedom, and even then their rights and privileges would be severely limited.

A historic marker near Jamestown, which can be seen on the next page, denotes the arrival of the "First Africans in Virginia." They were natives of Angola, kidnapped by Portuguese traders. They were loaded onto a ship headed for Veracruz in the colony of New Spain, where about 150 of the 350 died during transport—unfortunately, not an uncommon statistic. Then that ship was attacked by two other privateer ships, one being the *White Lion*. Both took some of the captives. The *White Lion* eventually docked at the Virginia Colony's Point Comfort, where the sailors traded twenty or so of the slaves for food.

Ironically, the first child of one of the African couples in Virginia was born a freeman under the law of that time. Before long, however, the demand for slaves increased and slavery became the law. Between the early 1500s and mid-1800s, an estimated twelve million Africans were taken to the New World. Approximately four hundred thousand went to North America, a small percentage compared to the five million shipped to Brazil and three million to the Caribbean.[22]

In 2015, Virginia's Department of Historic Resources posted this marker outside Fort Monroe to commemorate the 1619 arrival of the first Africans to the state.

Slave trading was a dangerous yet lucrative business for the traders, but it was merciless and brutal for those being transported. Traders resorted to inhumane means to get as many slaves onto a ship as possible. They would literally stack people below deck with men on one side of the ship, women on the other side, and sometimes children in the middle. That's right: They even transported children for slavery to the United States. Whenever a captive needed to urinate or defecate, or whenever the women were going through their monthly cycles, they had to do it right where they were. They were forced to live in their own soiled clothes, and many of them became sick as a result.

---

22   "First Enslaved Africans Arrive in Jamestown, Setting the Stage for Slavery in North America," History.com, https://www.history.com/this-day-in-history/first-african-slave-ship-arrives-jamestown-colony.

The shippers were not reimbursed for any of their captives who died during crossings. However, they *could* submit claims for slaves who drowned, so it became standard practice to throw overboard any slave who became seriously ill, allowing the shippers to be reimbursed for that lost slave. One small consolation of this heartless act was that it helped minimize sicknesses from running through the ship because everybody was chained so closely together. But the motive was profit, not the common good.

According to the Regulated Slave Trade Act of 1788, the British slave ship Brookes *could legally carry between 400-500 slaves.*

One British ship, similar to the illustration above, called the *Zong* sailed for the Americas in 1781 with 470 slaves on board. The crew would later testify that when the water supply ran low, they threw 130 of the slaves overboard. When they arrived in Jamaica, the slave traders filed a claim to be reimbursed for their losses. The court initially agreed to pay, but a legislator at the time filed charges that the slave traders should be charged with murder for those 130 deaths. The defense's argument, however, revealed the low esteem most people held toward Black people: "What is this claim that human people have been thrown overboard? This is a case of chattels or goods. Blacks are goods and property; it is madness to accuse these well-serving honourable men of murder. . . . The case is the same as if wood had been thrown overboard."[23]

The London high court eventually decided that the traders could not be charged with murder because what they threw overboard was no more than cargo. People from Africa were not even considered human! However, this atrocity attracted so much negative publicity that soon Parliament passed their first law to begin to regulate slave trading, the Slave Trade Act of 1788.

Marine biologists have noted that during the height of slave trading, sharks adapted their usual feeding patterns to follow the slave ships because so many captives were either thrown overboard or voluntarily jumped to their deaths to avoid further abuse and a future of enslavement. Published records have been found describing how at times the sharks would circle the ships, waiting for their next meal.

Not surprisingly, by the time slaves arrived in the New World, they were in very poor condition. In addition to the harsh travel conditions

During their transatlantic passage, many slaves were beaten and left permanently disfigured.

23   Ian Bernard, "The Zong Massacre (1781)," *BlackPast*, Oct. 11, 2011, https://www.blackpast.org/global-african-history/zong-massacre-1781/.

and rampant illnesses, many were also beaten. In the illustration on page 60, a man's entire back is covered with deep scars from being repeatedly whipped with a cat-o'-nine-tails, a barbarous instrument with bits of metal and glass embedded in the whip's knotted cords to rip into the victim's skin. And the captives often did not get much better treatment after they arrived and were sold.

This picture of slavery rightly makes people uncomfortable. It became common for defenders of slavery to portray the system as a cordial relationship between master and slave. Some even suggested that slavery was beneficial because it allowed Blacks to become educated and civilized, but if that were ever the case, it was the exception and not the rule. If such examples existed, they were very rare indeed. Slaves were owned property, so their children automatically became owned property as well. If they had an abusive owner and tried to escape, they could have their feet cut off. If they stole something, they could have their hand cut off. If they tried to get something to eat at an unscheduled time, they could be accused of stealing. It was a very rough and difficult life to live—if they managed to live through it. Few lived long lives because when they got older, they ceased to be as profitable for the master.

ALL MEN ARE CREATED EQUAL?

Americans take pride in our Declaration of Independence and its emphatic insistence that all men are created equal. Of course, that did not include people of color. We will see shortly that Black men were not even counted as whole people. Yet early drafts of the Declaration included a paragraph that at least stated that slave trading was wrong. The language of the time is a bit difficult to comprehend, but among the colonists' list of grievances against King George III and Great Britain was a longer paragraph that contained this section:

> He has waged cruel war against human nature itself, violating its most sacred rights of life and liberty in the persons of a distant people who never offended him, captivating & carrying them into slavery in

another hemisphere or to incur miserable death in their transportation thither. This piratical warfare, the opprobrium of infidel powers, is the warfare of the Christian King of Great Britain. Determined to keep open a market where Men should be bought & sold, he has prostituted his negative for suppressing every legislative attempt to prohibit or restrain this execrable commerce.[24]

By criticizing King George III for his participation in slave trading, the Declaration of Independence *almost* condemned the practice in 1776. But at the last minute, the Second Continental Congress removed this paragraph, which can be seen below, while making dozens of other edits. Thomas Jefferson would later say that this section was "struck out in complaisance to South Carolina & Georgia, who had never attempted to restrain the importation of slaves." However, Jefferson himself owned 180 slaves at the time.[25]

Even though Jefferson and the Second Continental Congress failed to hold Great Britain accountable for slave trading, forces within England were working for change. The previously mentioned *Zong* incident had captured the attention of many of Parliament's notables. One member, Sir William Dolben, described the awful treatment of slaves chained together and stowed like "herrings in a barrel" and afflicted with "putrid and fatal disorders."[26] He even organized a tour of a slave ship for his peers, resulting in the involvement of Prime Minister William Pitt and abolitionist William Wilberforce. The result was the Dolben Act, or the Slave Trade Act of 1788. It did not eliminate slave trading but began to regulate the practice to require more humane conditions during transportation. It was a small

---

24   "(1776) The Deleted Passage of the Declaration of Independence," *BlackPast*, Aug. 10, 2009, https://www.blackpast.org/african-american-history/declaration-independence-and-debate-over-slavery/.

25   Peter Kelley, "Documents That Changed the World: The Declaration of Independence's Deleted Passage on Slavery, 1776," *UW News*, Feb. 25, 2016, https://www.washington.edu/news/2016/02/25/documents-that-changed-the-world-the-declaration-of-independences-deleted-passage-on-slavery-1776/#:~:text=The%20deleted%20words%20%E2%80%94%20beginning%20with,his%20participation%20in%20and%20perpetuation.

26   "The 1788 Dolben Act," *Spartacus Educational*, https://spartacus-educational.com/REdolbenAct.htm.

step—but a start. The Act had to be renewed each year but was finally made permanent in 1799.

The United States was beginning to take some small steps of its own. Slave trading had been becoming more of a controversial issue. For much of the seventeenth century, the number of enslaved Africans was far less than European indentured servants in

This woodcut appeared on the 1837 publication of the American Quaker poet and abolitionist John Greenleaf Whittier's poem Our Countrymen in Chains.

the British colonies in North America. But as the flow of indentured servants sharply declined, the African slave trade saw a substantial increase. By the mid-eighteenth century, all thirteen colonies used slaves. Yet in January 1807, Congress passed an act, with support of Southern and Northern representatives, to "prohibit the importation of slaves into any port or place within the jurisdiction of the United States . . . from any foreign kingdom, place, or country."[27]

However, do not confuse slave trading with slavery. This act simply prevented further importing of slaves. Already, though, a population of more than four million enslaved people were scattered throughout New England and the South, and it was still

---

27   "Congress Abolishes the African Slave Trade," History.com, Dec. 4, 2020, https://www.history.com/this-day-in-history/congress-abolishes-the-african-slave-trade.

okay to sell or trade them. And since the children of slaves also became slaves, the South had a self-sustaining source of labor.

After the Revolutionary War, many of the Northern states began to pass laws to abolish slavery. Their economy was fueled by factories and manufacturing. Most farms were small, with little need for a large labor force. But the South was covered with sprawling farms and plantations. When the cotton gin was invented in 1793, the processing of cotton became a much more profitable venture and was the country's leading export by the mid-nineteenth century. The slogan of the times was "Cotton is king!" Yet even though much of the difficulty and tedium of removing the seeds from the cotton fiber had been eliminated, the planting and harvesting of the crops required much labor, and the South was unwilling to consider freeing all the slaves who provided that free manpower. Differences over slavery would create escalating conflicts between North and South.

One such conflict arose during the Constitutional Convention of 1787. James Madison had noted that "the States were divided into different interests not by their . . . size . . . but principally from their having or not having slaves." What the issue boiled down to was representation in Congress. When figuring population totals, some delegates favored representation based on the total number of inhabitants in a state, whether free or enslaved. Although the South was not willing to free its slaves, it wanted them to be counted. Others strongly disagreed because even free Blacks were not able to vote, and to include them in congressional representation would be paramount to encouraging the slave trade.

This conflict was eventually resolved with the "Three-fifths Compromise." It was determined that "three-fifths of the number of slaves in any particular state would be added to the total number of free white persons, including bond servants, but not Indians, to the estimated number of congressmen each state would send to the House of Representatives." The three-fifths clause was written into

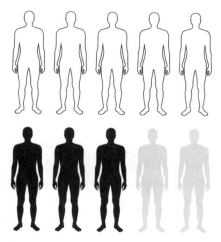

the United States Constitution. One result of this compromise was that for the entire period before the Civil War, slave-holding states had disproportionate influence on the Presidency, the Speakership of the House of Representatives, and the US Supreme Court.[28]

Some constitutional scholars take great umbrage if people interpret this decision to mean that African Americans were only considered three-fifths of a person because the fraction was used as an equalizing ratio. But from a Black perspective, it was really worse than that. Being acknowledged as three-fifths of a person, as illustrated above, would have been an improvement at the time because most owners of enslaved people did not consider them to be human at all. They were still treated like any other article of property. Suddenly, they got noticed so they could increase Southern representation in Congress, and the lawmakers in the South were trying to perpetuate slavery. It is still painful to consider how Black people were perceived during this era—and it was even more insulting for Native Americans! They were here before any of the Europeans came flooding into the country, and then as new documents were drafted to promote

28   M. Simba, "The Three-Fifths Clause of the United States Constitution (1787)," *BlackPast*, Oct. 3, 2014, https://www.blackpast.org/african-american-history/three-fifths-clause-united-states-constitution-1787/.

national freedom and equality, the original settlers were ignored and dismissed as being insignificant.

RACISM TOWARD ANOTHER GROUP

This would not be the biggest insult to Native Americans, however. Our discussion of race has focused on African Americans so far, but here is an example of egregious racism with a different culture. As white Europeans continued to come to America and populations swelled, the already-settled natives became a problem of inconvenience for growth-oriented immigrants. A policy had been established to respect the rights of the American Indians, but the rapid settlement of land east of the Mississippi River began to result in conflicts with indigenous peoples who were already settled. The situation was exacerbated when gold was found on Cherokee land in Georgia in 1828. Within two years, the Indian Removal Act of 1830 was passed. President Andrew Jackson had been emphatically pushing a new proposal to provide unsettled land on the Western prairies in exchange for the existing tribal lands in the East.

Some of the Northern tribes made the move with little resistance. But the Five Civilized Tribes in the Southeast (Chickasaw, Choctaw, Seminole, Cherokee, and Creek) rejected Jackson's proposed deal. They were called the civilized tribes because they had done everything requested of them in trying to get along with the European newcomers. They learned to speak and read English. They modeled land ownership and other lifestyle practices after white Americans. Many converted to Christianity. Some even had slaves! They not only had homes and a long history in that area, but they also had their children in missionary schools, their own representative government, and trades that contributed to the community. They were not just farmers who could easily move from one plot of land to another.

Yet when the Southern tribes refused to move voluntarily, the US Military was dispatched to force them out. State governments supported the federal government's efforts to move the Native Americans, yet when the legality of the move was questioned and taken to court, the case (*Worcester v. Georgia* [1832]) went to the

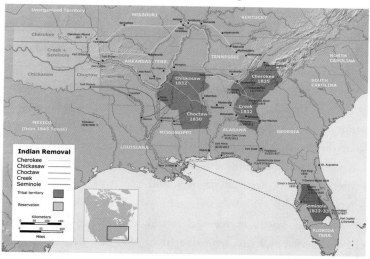

Supreme Court. The Court ruled in favor of the native nations, declaring that they were sovereign nations "in which the laws of Georgia [and other states] can have no force." Yet the ruling made no difference for the Native Americans when President Jackson refused to enforce it. As further incentive for them to leave, their white "neighbors" began to squat on their land, steal their livestock, loot and burn their homes and entire towns, and sometimes even slaughter the natives en masse.

When resistance proved futile, the Choctaw was the first nation to be completely removed in 1831. The tribe members were forced to march on foot for five thousand miles across what are now nine states, from North Carolina to Oklahoma. Some were chained, and the government provided no food or supplies. Thousands died along the way from disease, exposure, malnutrition, and exhaustion. A Choctaw leader commented that it was a "trail of tears and death." This "Trail of Tears" would be traveled for another decade as tribe after tribe was expelled, although the term is most often associated with the Cherokees, who suffered great losses during their forced departure.[29] Using military and tribal records, the estimate of total Native Americans forced to move was about one hundred thousand, with probably fifteen thousand dying along the way.[30]

How ironic (and distressing) it is that the term "Indian giver" came to mean someone who gives you something and then takes it back. Whoever coined that term must have had a sick sense of humor or been clueless about the facts. The Native Americans kept the treaties they made with the United States government, but those treaties would be repeatedly broken by the government leaders. A more accurate term would be "American giver"—at least, during this era of American history. While we are focusing on Black history to better understand how racism has been an ongoing problem, let us remember that other ethnicities had similar struggles and tragedies to contend with.

Just as white slave owners came to justify slavery by defining African Americans as "cargo" or "property," white settlers rationalized their mistreatment of Native Americans by labeling them "heathens." Yet even after tribes converted to Christianity and became better educated and more morally responsible than many of their white neighbors, the whites had no problem driving the natives off their ancestral property if they could make a financial gain by doing so.

MANIFEST DESTINY

As settlers moved farther and farther West, they justified their continued acquisition of tribal lands by bringing God into the picture:

---

29 "Trail of Tears," History.com, July 7, 2020, https://www.history.com/topics/native-american-history/trail-of-tears.

30 Elizabeth Prine Pauls, "Trail of Tears," *Encyclopaedia Britannica*, https://www.britannica.com/event/Trail-of-Tears.

Independence had been won in the Revolution and reaffirmed in the War of 1812. The spirit of nationalism that swept the nation in the next two decades demanded more territory. . . . Now, with territory up to the Mississippi River claimed and settled and the Louisiana Purchase explored, Americans headed west in droves. Newspaper editor John O'Sullivan coined the term "Manifest Destiny" in 1845 to describe the essence of this mindset.

The religious fervor spawned by the Second Great Awakening created another incentive for the drive west. Indeed, many settlers believed that God himself blessed the growth of the American nation. The Native Americans were considered heathens. By Christianizing the tribes, American missionaries believed they could save souls and they became among the first to cross the Mississippi River. . . .

At the heart of Manifest Destiny was the pervasive belief in American cultural and racial superiority. Native Americans had long been perceived as inferior, and efforts to "civilize" them had been widespread since the days of John Smith and Miles Standish. The Hispanics who ruled Texas and the lucrative ports of California were also seen as "backward."

Expanding the boundaries of the United States was in many ways a cultural war as well. The desire of southerners to find more lands suitable for cotton cultivation would eventually spread slavery to these regions. North of the Mason-Dixon line, many citizens were deeply concerned about adding any more slave states. Manifest Destiny touched on issues of religion, money, race, patriotism, and morality. These clashed in the 1840s as a truly great drama of regional conflict began to unfold.[31]

Manifest Destiny was the belief that it was the will of God for the United States to spread from the East coast to the West coast. It was a divine order. In exchange for taking the land from whomever was already there, we would be bringing knowledge, technology, and progress. Artist John Gast created a memorable painting to illustrate the Manifest Destiny mentality of the nation.

---

31   "Manifest Destiny," U.S. History, https://www.ushistory.org/us/29.asp.

Although his *American Progress*, which is pictured on page 71, was not painted until 1872, it captures the mindset of the pioneers of the 1840s. In the foreground (in the air) is Columbia, a female representation of the United States. (She would eventually be replaced by the Statue of Liberty and Uncle Sam.) She is moving west, stringing telegraph line with one hand as she goes. In the other hand, she holds a book. Beneath and around her are the prairies, rivers, and mountains. Before her goes a soon-to-be-outdated Conestoga wagon. Behind her come trains and a stagecoach. As she leads the way for the newcomers, American Indians and bison are running to get out of the way.

The *American Progress* painting, like the concept of Manifest Destiny itself, was designed to inspire pride in our growing country. However, America was almost entirely, in the terminology of the time, an Anglo-Saxon country. The growing conflict over slavery went west with the settlers, and the disregard for and mistreatment of Native Americans was displayed time and time again in different locations with different tribes. Although the United States saw itself as the godly proponents of progress, it was guilty of doing terrible, ungodly things during this period.

Even as slavery was spreading into the West, it was being debated in Washington, DC. We saw earlier that *legal* slave trade finally was terminated in 1807 with an act signed by Thomas Jefferson. It went into effect the next year, 1808, the same year Great Britain passed legislation to prohibit slave trading. The laws did not address the *practice* of slavery, but they supposedly prohibited further importing of slaves into the United States. However, not everyone adhered to the law, and the lucrative slave trade continued for a while. It is believed that one-fourth of all slaves that arrived in the United States got here *after* 1808. So although slave trade was illegal, the laws were rarely enforced.

Artist John Gast created this painting to illustrate the Manifest Destiny mentality of the nation. Although his American Progress *was not painted until 1872, it captures the mindset of the pioneers of the 1840s.*

However, movements had arisen in Great Britain, the United States, and other parts of the world to oppose the slave trade *and* end slavery altogether. The abolitionist movement was growing. Many people and groups refused to condone slavery, and spoke up against it. In the United States, Congress worked to arrive at a compromise that would bring the two widely divided factions together before serious damage was done to the country.

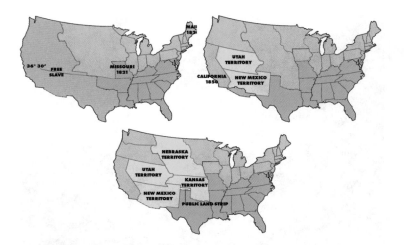

THE MISSOURI COMPROMISE OF 1820

In 1819, the United States had eleven free states and eleven slave states. The problem was that Missouri was requesting statehood, which would have swung the balance of power to the proslavery faction. Beyond that, the territories in the West that were approaching statehood had different opinions about slavery. Most everyone was pleased that the country was growing, but the problematic issues could no longer be avoided as had been done with the native tribes. Western expansion had all but ignored Native American rights. Few people in power noticed or cared enough to say much. The slavery issue was not going to go away, however, and the different opinions, strong on both sides, would not be easily resolved.

The Missouri Compromise attempted to maintain a balance of free states and slave states. Largely the plan of congressman Henry Clay, it established that anytime a slave state wanted to join the Union, a free state would join at the same time. Specifically, as Missouri joined as a slave state, Maine would join as a free state, maintaining a balance. However, that meant Missouri would become the northernmost of the existing slave states and the first state west of the Mississippi

River. Abolitionists become concerned because they did not want to see slavery push farther north or spread into the new and developing territories that were rapidly being populated. So the Compromise also stated from that time forward, slavery would be banned in all new lands north of 36° 30′ latitude (Missouri's southern border).[32]

Neither side was thrilled with this solution. Over time, everyone realized how difficult it would be to ensure an equal number of slave and free states, and the Compromise potentially eliminated the rights of certain new states to choose to practice slavery based simply on geographic location. Still, the Missouri Compromise lasted for more than thirty years.

THE COMPROMISE OF 1850

The Compromise of 1850 followed three decades later. After the Mexican-American War (1846–1848), the nation added new territories, and the conflict over slavery continued moving west. This act involved Henry Clay, Stephan Douglas, Daniel Webster, and John C. Calhoun, among others. It was comprised of five separate bills, among them the admission of California as a free state, the right of new territories to decide for themselves whether to permit slavery, and the addition of the Fugitive Slave Act of 1850 (a revival of one that had passed in 1793 but was not being enforced) that denied enslaved people the right to a trial by jury and required Northerners to assist in catching and returning runaway slaves. The Compromise of 1850 and especially the Fugitive Slave Act within it were met with strong opposition. Ironically, when Northerners refused to enforce it, the numbers of slaves moving north in search of freedom on the Underground Railroad *increased*. The acts were both repealed in 1864 after the Civil War broke out, since their intent had been to avoid that conflict.[33]

32   "Missouri Compromise," History.com, Nov. 4, 2019, https://www.history.com/topics/abolitionist-movement/missouri-compromise.

33   "Compromise of 1850," History.com, Feb. 10, 2020, https://www.history.com/topics/abolitionist-movement/compromise-of-1850.

THE KANSAS-NEBRASKA ACT OF 1854

The Kansas-Nebraska Act of 1854 effectively repealed the Missouri Compromise and expanded on one of the provisions of the Compromise of 1850. With all the new territories being developed (Utah Territory, New Mexico Territory, Kansas Territory, Nebraska Territory), the determination of "slave" vs. "free" states was no longer easy or convenient. Instead, it was decided that as states formed and joined the Union, the decision about slavery would be left up to each one. But by this time, increasing activism and political polarization had gotten beyond the point of a lasting compromise. It was a problem that proved unsolvable.

By the time Kansas joined the nation as a free state in January 1861, eight Southern states had already seceded. The nation was soon at war.[34]

I call this period of history the appeasement time. Instead of ending slavery and getting rid of the human atrocities it entailed, the government kept trying to find a way to compromise—to appease everyone and hold the Union together. But Congress was not going to keep the states united until they did something definitive about slavery. The inevitable result was the split that became the Civil War.

Why are we still off-base about race? Perhaps a big part of the problem is our history. Looking back, we have never had a model for what true equality between Blacks and whites can look like. Black people arrived as slaves and were not emancipated for 172 years (from 1691 until 1863), and as we will soon see, that was not the end of the injustices they suffered. For far too long, Black subjugation fell into the category of "the way things have always been" or even "God's will" for lots of people. After so much time and so much oppression, such history is not quickly forgotten. We still have not achieved equality, yet many people are currently working hard to create a society where, finally, all people are created (and treated) equal.

---

34 "Kansas-Nebraska Act," History.com, Aug. 27, 2019, https://www.history.com/topics/19th-century/kansas-nebraska-act.

5

The Flash Point
and the Explosion
(History: 1855–1875)

Before we continue our history lesson in this chapter, I would like to say how impressed I have been with the passion and zeal of young Black people who have gotten involved with civil rights and are fervently attempting to effect change in our society. However, in my experience, many of them may not have a clear understanding of their past. My goal, then, is to "connect the dots" between where we have been as a people and where we have arrived. Fervency and passion are admirable traits, but they are made even stronger when combined with knowledge. That is why I am focusing so much on history.

This chapter will cover an era of tremendous progress and hope for people of African descent. It looks as if things are really starting to go their way. The Emancipation Proclamation, the end of the Civil War, the Reconstruction Era, and some history-making amendments to the Constitution all point to an unprecedented time of positive change and opportunity. Enjoy this chapter while you can. Unfortunately, the mood will darken considerably in the next one.

DRED SCOTT

From the formation of the first Atlantic colonies in the United States, slavery was a fact of life. At first, slavery was not confined to the South. Even into the late 1700s, there were slaves in Maryland, New York, and other Northern colonies. But as Northerners were beginning to free their slaves, the South was having a widespread agricultural (and economic) boom. Slave owners were unwilling to release such an invaluable labor force for the intensive work required by crops like cotton and tobacco.

Debates were becoming more heated over how to regulate slavery in the newly forming Western states. The Republican Party was formed in the mid-1850s with a platform of opposition to extending slavery into the Western territories, but the Supreme Court confirmed the legality of slavery in those territories in the 1857 Dred Scott case. Scott was a slave who had been owned by different people and had lived in free states and territories at times. During a decade of lower-court trials, he had petitioned for and won his freedom at one point, but then had it revoked on appeal, and the Supreme Court had confirmed that decision. The high court ruled that whether free or enslaved, people of African descent were not United States citizens and therefore had no right to sue in federal court. Also, they said, the Fifth Amendment protected the rights of slave owners because the slaves were their legal property.[35]

It is difficult for modern people to comprehend what slavery was like in the eighteenth and early nineteenth centuries, even under the best of conditions. Enslaved couples were usually denied legal marriage, although Dred Scott married his wife, Harriet, in a civil ceremony, which was a rare exception. More typically, slaves adopted a "jumping the broom" ceremony that had originated in Ghana and was used not only in Africa but also by some other cultures, such as the Roma people (Gypsies). It was their way of showing commitment

---

35 "Dred Scott Case," History.com, Aug. 26, 2020, https://www.history.com/topics/black-history/dred-scott-case.

to one another and to God, even though they were not allowed a formal marriage ceremony.

African American families could never be confident they would stay together. Slaves could be sold or traded at the will of the owner. Parents could be separated from the rest of their family and never seen again. Children could be sold and taken away. They had been defined as property, and they were treated that way.

It is no wonder Dred Scott tried so intently to secure his freedom, yet he was denied in the end. His Supreme Court case was a victory for the proslavery faction and a blow to abolitionists, but it had attracted the attention of the nation.

LINCOLN, SECESSION, AND WAR

Abolitionist support was on the rise, and their new Republican party had a promising candidate, pictured right, in the upcoming 1860 election—Abraham Lincoln. Several Southern states had already threatened to secede if a Republican candidate won. In fact, South Carolina and Mississippi had been lobbying for secession since 1850. When Lincoln won the election in November, the South followed through with its threat. Seven states

The election of Republican Abraham Lincoln as the 16th president of the United States was the catalyst for the Southern states' secession from the Union.

had seceded by February 1861, forming the Confederate States of America and electing their own president—Jefferson Davis.

Troops on both sides gathered, and preparations were made for an inevitable conflict. On April 12, 1861, the Confederates overtook a Union stronghold, Fort Sumter in South Carolina, and the Civil War began. Four more states immediately joined the Confederacy, with others remaining sympathetic to the South and providing soldiers—but not formally seceding.

Many soldiers on both sides were eager to fight at first, wanting to defend their respective positions. But as the conflict ran on for years with troops and rations in short supply, and some of the bloodiest battles this country has known, the Civil War left the United States with scars that have not yet fully healed. Even this year, much effort has been made to set the record straight and remove many of the legacies that improperly glorify Southern leaders—statues, monuments, rebel flags, names of streets and buildings, etc. Although some people prefer to say that the Civil War was fought over the more respectable-sounding issue of "states' rights," few would deny that slavery was the root issue. Because one group of people was willing to die for the belief that they had the right to possess another group of people, our nation endured the costliest and deadliest war ever fought on American soil. Of the two million four hundred thousand soldiers involved, about six hundred twenty thousand of them were killed. Hundreds of thousands more were injured, and much of the South was left devastated.[36]

THE EMANCIPATION PROCLAMATION

Lincoln was elected as an abolitionist, but technically, he was not. When he was first elected, his views about slavery were still evolving. When the Declaration of Independence declared that "all men are

---

36 "Civil War," History.com, June 23, 2020, https://www.history.com/topics/american-civil-war/american-civil-war-history.

created equal," Lincoln took that to mean Black and white people alike should have the same social and political rights, yet he also believed the Constitution sanctioned slavery. He gave a three-hour speech in Peoria, Illinois, in 1854 that laid out those views. In 1858, during a series of debates, Stephen Douglas accused him of supporting "Negro equality." Lincoln clarified his position: "I will say then that I am not, nor ever have been, in favor of bringing about in any way the social and political equality of the white and Black races." He was against Black people having the right to vote, hold office, serve on juries, or intermarry with whites. Yet, he believed that all men had the right to improve their condition in society and enjoy the fruits of their labor. This, he thought, was true for both Blacks and whites, which was reason enough to oppose slavery.[37]

Yet after winning the election and then witnessing three years of brutal warfare, Lincoln wrote in April 1864: "I am naturally anti-slavery. If slavery is not wrong, nothing is wrong. I cannot remember when I did not so think, and feel."[38] His lingering question was what to do with the slaves if and when they were given their freedom. Should he free them and encourage them to return to their homeland in Liberia? Should he repeal slavery gradually, and if so, should slave owners be compensated for their losses? (I have read that Lincoln was considering a *very* gradual repeal of slavery—perhaps over a one-hundred-year period. If that had been the case, I very well might have been born a slave!)

History professor Eric Foner, author of *The Fiery Trial: Abraham Lincoln and American Slavery*, explains Lincoln's dilemma:

Lincoln is thinking through his own position on slavery. [His "Peoria speech"] really epitomizes his views into the Civil War. Slavery ought

---

37   Sarah Pruitt, "5 Things You May Not Know about Abraham Lincoln, Slavery and Emancipation," History.com, June 23, 2020, https://www.history.com/news/5-things-you-may-not-know-about-lincoln-slavery-and-emancipation.

38   "Letter to Albert G. Hodges," *Abraham Lincoln Online*, http://www.abrahamlincolnonline.org/lincoln/speeches/hodges.htm.

to be abolished—but he doesn't really know how to do it. He's not an abolitionist who criticizes Southerners. At this point, Lincoln does not really see black people as an intrinsic part of American society. They are kind of an alien group who have been uprooted from their own society and unjustly brought across the ocean. "Send them back to Africa," he says. And this was not an unusual position at this time . . .

The Emancipation Proclamation completely repudiates all of those previous ideas for Lincoln. [The abolishment of slavery is] immediate, not gradual. There is no mention of compensation and there is nothing in it about colonization. After the Emancipation Proclamation, Lincoln says nothing publicly about colonization.[39]

Lincoln's primary goal was to hold the Union together. His Emancipation Proclamation in 1863 did not do what many people today believe it did. It did not free all the slaves. It hardly freed any of them. Lincoln made his position clear in an 1862 newspaper editorial: "My paramount object in this struggle *is* to save the Union and is *not* either to save or to destroy slavery. If I could save the union without freeing *any* slave I would do it, and if I could save it by freeing *all* the slaves I would do it; and if I could save it by freeing some and leaving others alone I would also do that."[40]

Toward that goal, in September 1862 Lincoln had urged all Confederate states to rejoin the Union. He was giving them one hundred days, until January 1. If they did not respond, he would declare their slaves "thenceforward, and forever free." After no response, and following a decisive Union victory at Antietam, he issued the Emancipation Proclamation on January 1, 1863. But the freedom provided by that document was very limited. The Proclamation stated that as of that date, all enslaved people in the states *currently engaged in rebellion against the Union* would be freed. Even Lincoln's secretary of state,

---

39   "Lincoln's Evolving Thoughts on Slavery, and Freedom," Oct. 11, 2010, From NPR interview with Eric Foner, *The Fiery Trial: Abraham Lincoln and American Slavery* (New York: W. W. Norton & Company, 2010), https://www.npr.org/2010/10/11/130489804/lincolns-evolving-thoughts-on-slavery-and-freedom.

40   "Emancipation Proclamation," History.com, Sept. 18, 2020, https://www.history.com/topics/american-civil-war/emancipation-proclamation.

William Seward, was critical: "We show our sympathy with slavery by emancipating slaves where we cannot reach them and holding them in bondage where we can set them free."[41]

Yet the Emancipation Proclamation was a decisive turning point. For one thing, as the nation saw suddenly freed slaves flooding to the North as the Union armies worked their way to the South, it put to death the naïve presumption that many slaves were quite happy under the "protection" of their white owners. Almost two hundred thousand of those more than three million emancipated slaves immediately used their freedom to join the Union Army. In addition, Lincoln's commitment to free the slaves shifted much European support from the Confederacy to the Union.[42]

African Americans already had a proud tradition of defending the country that did not even consider them equal to the whites. When you examine war records, you can turn up some surprises: "Black Americans have served in every one of America's conflicts since the Revolutionary War. Since the Medal of Honor's inception, 88 African Americans have earned the distinction." The Medal of Honor was created for the Civil War, but in 1863, Congress had already made it a permanent decoration. Twenty-six Black soldiers received the medal during the Civil War—eighteen from the Army and eight from the Navy.[43]

Many African American churches still commemorate the Emancipation Proclamation on New Year's Eve. It was a giant step away from slavery toward freedom, but it was just a start. The years following the Proclamation would provide even better reasons to celebrate.

---

41   "Emancipation Proclamation," *Africans in America*, PBS, https://www.pbs.org/wgbh/aia/part4/4h1549.html.

42   "Emancipation Proclamation," History.com, Ibid.

43   Charles W. Hanna, African American Recipients of the Medal of Honor (Jefferson, NC: McFarland & Company, 2002), p. 3.

FROM APPOMATTOX TO JUNETEENTH

After four years of fighting, the Confederate states proved no match for the Union armies. General Robert E. Lee surrendered his troops to Ulysses S. Grant at Virginia's Appomattox Court House on April 9, 1865. This event is often portrayed as the final act of the Civil War, but Lee's surrender was only the first domino in the concession of the South to the North. In the weeks that followed, other Confederate generals made similar surrenders in the Carolinas, Alabama, and throughout the South. President Abraham Lincoln could see the war winding down, but he would not be able to celebrate its conclusion. He was assassinated on April 14, 1865.

The final land battle of the Civil War was the Battle of Palmito Ranch, near Brownsville, Texas, on May 12. However, Texas had been far removed from much of the hostility of the war. As Northern troops made more and more progress into the South, many plantation owners had fled to Texas with their slaves rather than release them or allow the Union Army to capture them. Consequently, there were more than 250,000 African Americans in Texas, still enslaved and largely unaware of the Emancipation Proclamation issued more than two years previously.

News was slow to reach Texas, but it eventually got there. On June 19, 1865, Major General Gordon Granger of the Union Army arrived in Galveston with two thousand Union troops and let everyone know the Civil War was over. Even better news for the quarter million slaves there, Granger publicly read an official order: "The people of Texas are informed that, in accordance with a proclamation from the Executive of the United States, all slaves are free."[44]

Not surprisingly, Granger's announcement sparked statewide celebrations throughout Texas. The date was commemorated with the annual acknowledgment of June 19, "Juneteenth," now the oldest

---

44   Tom Huddleston, Jr., "Juneteenth: The 155-Year-Old Holiday's History Explained," CNBC. com, June 17, 2020, https://www.cnbc.com/2020/06/15/what-is-juneteenth-holidays-history-explained.html.

nationally celebrated commemoration in the United States, celebrating the ending of slavery. Currently, several states are pushing to make it a national holiday.

THE THIRTEENTH AMENDMENT (1865)

The Emancipation Proclamation was the first ray of hope that Black Americans were on their way to freedom. The announcement in Texas on Juneteenth was another cause of celebration. But it was the Thirteenth Amendment to the Constitution, ratified on December 6, 1865, that gave official and lasting government sanction to that freedom:

> Neither slavery nor involuntary servitude, except as a punishment for crime whereof the party shall have been duly convicted, shall exist within the United States, or any place subject to their jurisdiction.

There it is. Finally. The official declaration that *really* set African Americans free. The first time the word *slavery* was used in the Constitution was to abolish it. Abraham Lincoln himself submitted this resolution to the state legislatures for ratification the day after it passed in the House of Representatives on January 31, but the required number of states did not ratify the amendment until December 6, so Lincoln never saw the end result.[45]

Before moving on, however, take another look at that "except as a punishment for crime" clause in this amendment. I will come back to that shortly and explain how that was used as a loophole by people and groups who were not as thrilled with the freedom and equality the amendment intended to provide.

---

45 "13th Amendment," History.com, June 9, 2020, https://www.history.com/topics/black-history/thirteenth-amendment.

THE RECONSTRUCTION ERA (1865–1877)

The years following the Civil War were a chaotic period for many people. As the divided nation began to begin to heal, many recently freed slaves and poor white Southerners found themselves without direction. Reconstruction promised to provide real hope and optimism as Black people began to gain official status through various official legislative actions, several of which are listed below.

Abraham Lincoln was already planning for a time of reconstruction less than a year after he gave the Emancipation Proclamation. He realized that a plan would be necessary to streamline the return to the Union of the states which had seceded, to provide a future for the newly freed slaves, and many other such details. But there was still much division even within the political spectrum. The abolitionists had come out ahead and were eager to legislate long-desired improvements, but there was still much opposition to total equality for freed slaves.

Perhaps you have heard comments along the lines of Reconstruction being a somewhat vindictive opportunity for the progressive abolitionists to impose their will on the defeated Southerners as well as some of their more moderate peers. That might have been true, to some extent. At least, that is what it likely felt like to those in the South. In retrospect, however, the effects of Reconstruction were seen in a much more positive light. It was a period that demonstrated what the country had been missing by blindly dismissing the potential contributions of African Americans to science, politics, and culture as a whole. We will soon see how Black people proved themselves equal as long as they were allowed to . . . and then how suddenly and totally that privilege was taken away from them.

THE BLACK CODES (1865–1866)

The pushback to Reconstruction happened immediately. Southern states could not reenter the Union and have any real opportunity to recover from the war until they renounced secession and abolished slavery. But aside from these requirements, state governments were relatively free to make their own decisions. They were not thrilled with the changes that were allowing freed slaves to flourish, and they were quick to respond.

Many of them immediately began to establish what became known as Black codes—only slightly modified versions of the old slave codes, enacted to regain a regular supply of cheap labor from the Black people they still saw as inferior. Former slaves could not testify against whites in court, could not carry guns, or have an interracial marriage (although marriage between African Americans was now legal.)

In addition, this is where proslavery advocates began to abuse the "exception clause" in the Thirteenth Amendment. The amendment had outlawed slavery, yes, *except* as punishment for someone convicted of a crime. This loophole led to widespread arrest of freed slaves for no legitimate reason. Law enforcement officers used an absurdly broad interpretation of vagrancy laws to justify an idle person's arrest, high fine, and term of labor when unable to pay it. If you did not have a job, you could be sent to jail. If you were standing on the corners, you could be sent to jail. If you were performing any kind of task deemed inappropriate (even if not necessarily illegal), you could be sent to jail. And if you were poor, as so many of them were, the only way you could get out of jail was to work off your fine—often on a chain gang or plantation. It was not uncommon for African Americans to find themselves trying to pay off a fine for a trumped-up charge by working for their former owner on the same farm.[46]

Many of the policemen and judges were former Confederate soldiers, so getting a fair trial or sentence was highly unlikely. In addition, the Black codes required African Americans to sign labor contracts each year and otherwise limited their options and freedom.

46   Amy McKenna, "Black Code," Britannica.com, Aug. 20, 2019, https://www.britannica.com/topic/black-code.

Even Lincoln's successor, President Andrew Johnson, endorsed the Black codes, but kept getting outvoted when he tried to promote his policies. The abuses perpetrated through these codes probably prompted the rapid passing of the Fourteenth Amendment.

Although members of the Ku Klux Klan kept their identities secret by wearing hoods and robes, it was common knowledge that membership covered the entire social spectrum.

THE RISE OF THE KU KLUX KLAN (FORMED 1865)

A more organized and sinister resistance took root in 1865 when a group in Pulaski, Tennessee, began a secret society. Taking a name believed to be derived from the Greek word for "circle" (*kyklos*), they became known as the Ku Klux Klan (KKK). Southern General Nathan Bedford Forrest was chosen to lead the group as "grand wizard." The group organized to resist the constitutional changes being made that required states to initiate and enforce "equal protection" to previously enslaved people. Even after Congress passed laws specifically intended to bring an end to Klan terrorism, their primary goal remained to reestablish white supremacy.

Their racist mentality found a lot of support in opposition to the Republican plans being instituted during Reconstruction. By 1870, the KKK had spread into almost every Southern state, joining forces with other white supremacist groups and celebrating Democratic victories in state elections throughout the South in the 1870s.

Opposition to Klan activities was unlikely to do any good and could possibly make the situation worse. As can be seen in the picture to the left, the hooded costumes of members kept their identities secret, yet it was common knowledge that membership included the whole social spectrum—small-time farmers, laborers, store owners, doctors, law enforcement officers, and even ministers.

The influence of the Ku Klux Klan has ebbed and flowed over the years. But because it was an organization rooted in racism, and because racism has never been eliminated from American culture, the Klan is still active, even today.[47]

THE FREEDMEN'S BUREAU (1865–1872)

As the ravages of war began to affect the South, Congress established the Bureau of Refugees, Freedmen, and Abandoned Lands. Better known as the Freedmen's Bureau, it was an organization designed to claim land that had been abandoned or confiscated during the war and put it to good use for poor whites and former slaves. The Bureau built hospitals and schools, fed millions of people, provided legal help (including helping former slaves legalize marriages), assisted Black veterans, and helped freed slaves find lost relatives. They wanted to redistribute the land to enable Southern Blacks to build homes, yet most of it was eventually returned to the original owners.

In many communities, Bureau agents were the only federal representatives. Although they were performing beneficial work, much like today's social workers, they were often met with resistance, whether in the form of ridicule or a more violent response. As opposition from white Southerners increased, the Freedmen's Bureau was hampered in its efforts by politics, insufficient personnel, and inadequate

47   "Ku Klux Klan," History.com, Nov. 2, 2020, https://www.history.com/topics/reconstruction/ku-klux-klan.

funding. However, Howard University was established in 1867 and named for Oliver Howard, one of its founders and presidents, and one-time head of the Freedmen's Bureau.

The Bureau is credited with getting the federal government involved in social issues like welfare and labor relations. One reporter noted: "The Bureau helped awaken Americans to the promise of freedom, and for a time, the Bureau's physical presence in the South made palpable to many citizens the abstract principles of equal access to the law and free labor."[48]

THE CIVIL RIGHTS ACT OF 1866

The Civil Rights Act of 1866 was proposed to grant citizenship to "all persons born in the United States"—except for American Indians. (More irony: Native Americans were the only ones not allowed to become American citizens.) This was the first legislation of civil rights in Congress, and the bill passed only after the House overrode two vetoes by President Andrew Johnson. Still, Blacks finally had the legal right to buy homes, own property, and become US citizens.[49]

THE FOURTEENTH AMENDMENT (1868)

In the 1857 Dred Scott case, the Supreme Court had said that even Black people who were born free were not able to claim citizenship. The Fourteenth Amendment redefined citizenship in the United States: "All persons born or naturalized in the United States and subject to the jurisdiction thereof, are citizens of the United States and of the State wherein they reside."

48   "Freedmen's Bureau," History.com, Oct. 3, 2018, https://www.history.com/topics/black-history/freedmens-bureau#:~:text=The%20Freedmen's%20Bureau%2C%20formally%20known,aftermath%20of%20the%20Civil%20War.

49   "The Civil Rights Bill of 1866," *History, Art & Archives*, United States House of Representatives, https://history.house.gov/Historical-Highlights/1851-1900/The-Civil-Rights-Bill-of-1866/.

This amendment also clarified that "No state shall make or enforce any law which shall abridge the privileges or immunities of citizens of the United States." It was no longer left up to individual states to determine the status of African Americans. The rights of Black people were to be protected by both federal and state governments.

THE FIFTEENTH AMENDMENT (1870)

The Fourteenth Amendment allowed African Americans (and others) to become United States citizens. The Fifteenth Amendment gave them the most basic privilege of citizenship—the right to vote. "The right of citizens of the United States to vote shall not be denied or abridged by the United States or by any State on account of race, color, or previous condition of servitude."

This right, however, was still limited to males at the time. It would be another half-century before women—Black or white—were legally allowed to vote. But Black men put this privilege to good use. They joined with the Republicans who had supported their advancement, and by the time the Confederate states rejoined the Union, most of them were under Republican control.

All too soon, however, control would shift and white supremacists would impose all sorts of regulations to complicate or prevent voting for people of African descent: poll taxes, literacy tests, and so forth. It would not be until the 1965 Voting Rights Act that all these barriers were removed and forbidden.

THE CIVIL RIGHTS ACT OF 1875

The Civil Rights Act of 1875 was written with the intent of outlawing outright racial discrimination in public places such as buses and trains, juries, schools, theaters, and so forth. However, another move was growing to promote segregation instead, and proponents of the bill had to soften the language and make so many concessions to get it passed that it failed to make much of a difference for Black people.[50] It would soon be revoked.

Al Jolson (above) in The Jazz Singer—*the first talking picture produced in the United States. Thomas Dartmouth Rice (right) performed a caricature of a slave in his minstrel show popular throughout the South in the 19th century.*

JIM CROW LAWS (1876)

The Black codes that began in 1865 evolved into the Jim Crow laws—an even more aggressive set of state and local laws that legalized racial segregation. The name Jim Crow came from the minstrel show character pictured above, Jumping Jim Crow, played by an actor who dressed in blackface. He would put black polish on his face and entertain crowds by making fun of the way Black people interacted and talked to each other. His act was offensive to Blacks, as were these laws.

Jim Crow laws denied to African Americans basic rights which they had already been given—holding a job, getting an education, voting, and so forth. But it was not the legal system that was enforcing these corrupted "laws." Anyone who tried to ignore them risked arrest, fines, jail, or worse. Some were beaten; others were killed. As

---

50   "The Civil Rights Act of 1875," *History, Art & Archives*, United States House of Representatives, https://history.house.gov/Historical-Highlights/1851-1900/The-Civil-Rights-Act-of-1875/ and "Civil Rights Act of 1875 Declared Unconstitutional," Annenberg Classroom. https://www.annenbergclassroom.org/timeline_event/civil-rights-act-of-1875-declared-unconstitutional/.

time passed, they became more and more restrictive, and they created a lot of sorrow, pain, and division until they were officially ended with the Civil Rights Act of 1964.[51] And even then, the spirit of Jim Crow continued to influence Black esteem and racial equality.

Despite the introduction of the Black codes, the Jim Crow laws, and the formation of the Ku Klux Klan, the Reconstruction Era was an amazing time for the newly freed African Americans. When they joined their votes with those of progressive Republicans, the South saw unprecedented change:

> [Reconstruction] was essentially a large-scale experiment in interracial democracy unlike that of any other society following the abolition of slavery. Southern Black people won election to southern state governments and even to the US Congress during this period. Among the other achievements of Reconstruction were the South's first state-funded public school systems, more equitable taxation legislation, laws against racial discrimination in public transport and accommodations, and ambitious economic development programs (including aid to railroads and other enterprises).[52]

Yes, you read that right. Only five years after the Civil War, a Black man was sworn in as a senator from Mississippi. That honor went to Hiram Revels in 1870. Blanche K. Bruce was the second, in 1875. A total of two thousand or so African Americans served in other government positions during Reconstruction: sixteen in the US Congress, more than six hundred in state legislatures, and hundreds more in local positions across the South—yet these numbers still were not representative of their population.[53]

How long would you guess it took to elect the third Black senator? Sadly, it would be almost a century until Edward Brooke was

---

51   "Jim Crow Laws," History.com, Dec. 2, 2020, https://www.history.com/topics/early-20th-century-us/jim-crow-laws.

52   "Emancipation and Reconstruction," History.com, Nov. 2, 2020, https://www.history.com/topics/american-civil-war/reconstruction.

53   "Black Leaders During Reconstruction," History.com, Dec. 10, 2020, https://www.history.com/topics/american-civil-war/black-leaders-during-reconstruction.

elected in 1967. And when the first female African American senator, Carol Moseley Braun, was elected in 1993, she was only the fourth. Barack Obama would become the fifth in 2005. Kamala Harris, our new vice president, was number ten. So despite the optimism of the Reconstruction Era, progress for Black Americans has been slow since then.[54]

The political climate took a drastic, and for African Americans, a heartbreaking turn in the late 1870s. Here is how one historian summarized the situation:

> By the turn of the century, a new racial system had been put in place in the South, resting on the disenfranchisement of Black voters, a rigid system of racial segregation, the relegation of African Americans to low-wage agricultural and domestic employment, and legal and extra-legal violence to punish those who challenged the new order. Nonetheless, while flagrantly violated, the Reconstruction amendments remained in the Constitution, sleeping giants, as Charles Sumner called them, to be awakened by subsequent generations who sought to redeem the promise of genuine freedom for the descendants of slavery. Not until the 1960s, in the civil rights movement, sometimes called the "second Reconstruction," would the country again attempt to fulfill the political and social agenda of Reconstruction.[55]

What happened? We will move on to those disheartening events in the next chapter, but first we need to pause and reflect for a few moments on what might have been. When you consider the rapid and immediate progress that was made when African Americans were allowed to have equal opportunity, you see how much potential was there which had never been acknowledged. No sooner had they been freed from servitude on farms or plantations than many stepped into jobs of responsibility and respect. They were improving the social welfare of their communities. It was a very promising and optimistic time.

---

54   "African American Senators," United States Senate, https://www.senate.gov/pagelayout/history/h_multi_sections_and_teasers/Photo_Exhibit_African_American_Senators.htm.

55   Eric Foner, "Reconstruction," Britannica.com, Sept. 10, 2020, https://www.britannica.com/event/Reconstruction-United-States-history.

I have to wonder how our country might be different today if that kind of progress had continued. What might God have done to bring about healing, to bring about a sense of equality, if the people in power had not been so resistant? And what are the lessons for us today?

This was more than a period of struggle and frustration for African Americans; it was a fight for the souls of people. I believe God has been present in this ongoing struggle, urging righteous people to intercede and fight for the liberty of others who are not yet free. He certainly wants us to be free spiritually and able to enjoy a growing relationship with Him, but it is also important to be free socially and treat one another fairly while we are in this world. However, throughout this long struggle for civil rights and equality, many people have resisted allowing African Americans to achieve a level of civic freedom. Many have fought diligently to stop it from occurring. The fact that some still do is a sad and troubling thought.

Why are we still off-base about race? Throughout history, the sad truth has been that the equality that some people and groups seek—and deserve—can be threatening to those in power. The next few chapters will show some of the extreme lengths to which some white people and groups have gone to prevent Black people from their legitimate (and constitutional) rights.

6

The Shattered Promise
(History: 1876–1910)

isputed elections and manipulative political strategies are not new to the twenty-first century. If you think the 2020 election was combative, contentious, and messy, you should have been around in 1876. Political tensions had been building since the end of the Civil War. The Southern states had been readmitted to the Union by then, but the Democratic Party's attitudes hadn't changed much from prewar thinking, and the Republican Party was divided. The progressive Republicans did not think Lincoln's policies, in his effort to restore the Union, had sufficiently penalized the rebellious Southerners. Despite the success stories of African Americans in society and politics during Reconstruction, at war's end, most were still uneducated, dirt poor, and mistreated.

Lincoln's successor, Andrew Johnson, had taken an even more liberal political position. As a Tennessee congressman, governor, and senator, he had owned slaves, yet he was strongly opposed to secession. When Lincoln was elected, he changed parties and became a Republican. After Tennessee seceded, he was the only Southern senator who stayed in the Senate and refused to join the Confederacy. He remained loyal to the Union, yet he was never an advocate for the freed slaves, once stating, "Damn the negroes, I am fighting those traitorous aristocrats, their masters."[56]

As president, Johnson pardoned most Southern whites for their rebellion, excluding only Confederate leaders—although most of them were eventually pardoned on an individual basis. As the new Southern state governments were being formed, the only requirements he imposed were the repayment of their war debt, the abolishment of slavery, and a disavowal of secession. Otherwise, they were free to determine their own rules and regulations, but that was easier said than done. The situation in the South was dire:

> There were large areas of great devastation, rubbled cities, neglected farms, hunger, a fractured and demoralized society in chaos, with hundreds of thousands of internally displaced persons (including newly-freed slaves and soldiers just released from the disbanded Confederate Army), and little remaining civil government. In short, there was little—beyond the Union Army—to prevent the entire region from slipping away into post-war anarchy. . . . The specifics of how they did this varied, but a closer look at the situation in the fallen capital of the Confederacy, Richmond, Virginia, offers a good example. . . .
>
> Perhaps the most immediate task with long-term implications was the restoration of agriculture. There were only a few weeks left to plant crops for the growing season and the fields around Richmond were greatly neglected. The situation was not only a matter of tending the fields and doing the planting; it also involved labor issues—the slaves were now freedmen, and their labor was no longer mandatory or free. The Army had to assume the role of jobs bureau and facilitate a new relationship that could get the crops planted while protecting the rights of former slaves. To encourage freedmen to return to the farms they had previously worked, the Army tied distribution of food rations for able-bodied workers to their willingness to work. At the same time, the Army had to ensure that the landowners paid these returning workers appropriately (sometimes even designating what that wage should be) and treated them as the freemen they now were.[57]

---

56 "Andrew Johnson," *Britannica*, https://www.britannica.com/biography/Andrew-Johnson.

57 Lieutenant Colonel Jeffrey A. Calvert, "The Occupation of the South," *Army Heritage Center Foundation*, https://www.armyheritage.org/soldier-stories-information/the-occupation-of-the-south/.

As we saw in the previous chapter, Reconstruction had been a boon to African Americans. It was clear, however, that not everyone was at ease with the rapid increase of status and prominence of Blacks in society and politics. Southern states adopted the Black codes, and the Ku Klux Klan began to grow in strength and numbers. Yet those demeaning influences were being held at bay to some extent, thanks to federal troops that had been deployed to keep the peace.

Johnson's presidency continued to complicate African American progress because he feared what might happen if Blacks were given power over whites. He attempted to veto the Civil Rights Act of 1866, but the veto was overridden by Congress. He did succeed in vetoing a bill that would have extended the Freedman's Bureau, leading to the closing of that institution. He opposed the Fourteenth Amendment that granted citizenship and equal protection under the law to slaves (or anyone) born in the United States, but it was ratified anyway.

Johnson was replaced in 1869 by Ulysses S. Grant who, like Lincoln, was intent on reuniting the North and the South. He had been in favor of pardoning Confederate leaders, yet he also promoted legislature and policies that advanced the civil rights of former slaves. But as happens so often when compromise is attempted, neither side is really satisfied. Some people accused Grant of interfering with states' rights, and other said he had not gone far enough to ensure the new freedom and equality of African Americans. But since Grant had stationed federal troops throughout the South to ensure law and order, the power of groups like the Ku Klux Klan was limited.[58] It was during Grant's two terms that the freed slaves began to find success and acceptance in an increasingly integrated culture.

---

[58] "Ulysses S. Grant," History.com, March 30, 2020, https://www.history.com/topics/us-presidents/ulysses-s-grant-1.

THE COMPROMISE OF 1877 /
THE END OF RECONSTRUCTION

So what ended Reconstruction? Political tensions reached whole new levels with the presidential election of 1876. Rutherford B. Hayes, the Republican candidate, was running against Samuel Tilden for the Democrats. By midnight of election night that November, Tilden had 184 electoral votes, needing only one more to win, and he was ahead by 250,000 in the popular vote. However, all the remaining votes were being disputed.

Republican influence in the South had been declining throughout the 1870s. By the 1876 election, only three Southern states still had Republican governors, and Republicans accused Democrats of intimidation and bribery to prevent African Americans from voting in those states. Indeed, the South Carolina election had been marked by violence and bloodshed. Along with Florida and Louisiana, the three states had submitted two sets of election returns with differing results. Meanwhile, the Democratic governor of Oregon had replaced a Republican elector with a Democrat, putting that crucial vote in jeopardy. Now what?

Congress decided to establish an electoral commission that would be as fair as possible. It included five members of the House of Representatives, five senators, and five Supreme Court justices. Among the chosen group, seven were Democrats, seven were Republicans, and one was an independent. But when the independent declined to serve, he was replaced with a Republican.

So even as the commission was meeting, the Republicans met with moderate Democrats to strike a deal. It was agreed that the Democrats would cede the victory to Hayes and respect the civil and political rights of African Americans. In exchange, Hayes would agree to placing a leading Southerner in his cabinet, support federal aid for the Texas and Pacific Railroad, and withdraw all federal soldiers from the South.

On March 2, 1877, Rutherford B. Hayes officially received 185 votes, squeaking by with a victory. He appointed a Tennessean as postmaster general, but never followed through with his promise to help fund the railroad. He did, however, withdraw all federal troops who had been safeguarding the constitutional rights of Southern African Americans. The Southern Democrats immediately reneged on their promise to ensure the rights of Black citizens. That was the death blow to Reconstruction. The Jim Crow laws went into effect, and the South became strictly segregated.

African Americans still had *legal* rights, of course, but those rights were no longer being enforced. With the removal of military protection, Blacks were increasingly intimidated and threatened if they attempted to vote, seek employment, purchase homes, or hold property. The Compromise of 1877 completely changed the outlook for Black people in the South. They would not see a similar level of equality and respect for more than a century, until the Civil Rights Movement of the 1960s.[59]

THE CIVIL RIGHTS CASES OF 1883

It had looked as if the Reconstruction Era might become a long-awaited, liberating period of equality for Blacks and whites. It was a time when more people began to speak up for civil rights, but the voices of the opponents were louder and more persistent. In 1883, the US Supreme Court heard five cases that, because of their similarity, were consolidated into a single ruling.

Various individuals and groups had been pushing back on the Civil Rights Act of 1875. It was written to ensure fair treatment of African Americans in public places. But opponents had raised the question, "What about *private* places? Don't I have a say in who eats in my restaurant, gets on my bus, or sits in my movie theater?" The act forbade the federal government from discriminating, but what about private citizens? Such arguments were a blatant attempt to legalize prejudice, and the case went all the way to the Supreme Court. In an eight to one decision, the court ruled that if a state failed to enforce the laws and, by

---

59   "Compromise of 1877," History.com, https://www.history.com/topics/us-presidents/compromise-of-1877.

not acting, allowed discrimination, Congress had no right to step in and legislate. Not only did this remove congressional protection of African Americans provided in the Fourteenth Amendment, it also invited the Southern states to tolerate (and even encourage) private discrimination.

The one dissenting vote came from Judge John Marshall Harlan (named after John Marshall, another Supreme Court justice his parents had admired). At one point in his career, Harlan had been described as "a Southern gentleman and a slave-holder, and at heart a conservative." Although he fought in the Union Army and opposed secession, he had not been in favor of emancipating the slaves and then protecting them with civil rights laws. Yet after witnessing the brutality of Ku Klux Klan tactics, he underwent an immediate conversion, renounced his previous views, became a Republican, and was appointed to the Supreme Court by Rutherford B. Hayes in 1877.[60]

In the civil rights cases, Harlan had argued that if your privately owned establishment has an effect upon the public interest, then you no longer have a right to discriminate. His was a bold stand to take in 1883. I respect Harlan as an example of how God positions champions to promote righteousness, even when their voices are not heard, heeded, or popular. But despite Harlan's best efforts, the Civil Rights Act of 1875 was ruled unconstitutional, striking down the previous prohibition of racial discrimination in public places. More power was granted individual states in how to regulate private, informal, and local practices of racial segregation. This ruling would remain in force until it was corrected in the 1964 Civil Rights Act.[61]

That is right. *The Civil Rights Act of 1964 was essentially a rewrite of the Civil Rights Act of 1875, but it took almost a hundred years to replace it!* But we will not stop there. The Civil Rights Act of 1866, which gave newly freed African American slaves the right to own and

---

60   C. Vann Woodward, "Plessy v. Ferguson," *American Heritage*, Vol. 15, Issue 3, 1964, https://www.americanheritage.com/plessy-v-ferguson#1.

61   Melvin I. Urofsky, "Civil Rights Cases," *Britannica*, Oct. 8, 2020, https://www.britannica.com/topic/Civil-Rights-Cases.

transfer private property, was never honored and ended up being overlooked. Those rights were not relegislated until the Civil Rights Act of 1968 being signed in the picture. That means *two acts of Congress, both providing basic civil rights for Black Americans, had to be redone, but it took about a hundred years to replace them!*

We think the civil rights movement of the sixties was brand new. No. During that time, African Americans again received the rights that had been given—and then taken away—a century or so before.

Just think what might have been

President Lyndon B. Johnson signed the Civil Rights Act of 1968 on April 11, 1968—two days after the funeral of Dr. Martin Luther King Jr.

accomplished during that hundred-year period! During Reconstruction, African Americans had the right to vote, to hold elected office, and to buy and sell property. What is more important, those rights were protected and enforced, regardless of skin color.

Let me tell you what happens when you stop people from buying and owning property: You stop them from accumulating wealth. If whites are allowed to accumulate real estate and pass it along to their heirs while Blacks are not—over the course of a century—the financial inequality is significant. It is not surprising that hard feelings and tensions develop. (We will go into more detail about this in a later chapter.) African Americans were stopped during that hundred-year period from 1866 to 1968—a century of lost time until basic human rights were finally restored and honored.

However, as I hope to show you in the next few chapters, it is not appropriate to attribute the problem to a clear-cut Black vs. white issue. Caucasians as a group benefited from the unfair laws (and the lack of enforcement of fair ones), but that does not mean all white people approved. Just as there have always been racists who vehemently opposed equality for Blacks, there have also been white people throughout history who have promoted justice and civil rights for all people. They fought for equality then and still do now.

THE BIRTH OF EUGENICS (1883)

While the US Supreme Court was deliberating the Civil Rights Cases of 1883, across the Atlantic, Sir Francis Galton was publishing a new book, *Inquiries into Human Faculty and Its Development*. In that book, he coined the term *eugenics* ("good creation"), a concept built on Plato's speculation about designing a better society by encouraging procreation among upper-class, enlightened individuals and discouraging mating between lower classes. Ever since he put his thoughts to paper, the "science" of eugenics has been with us in one form or another—some far more insidious than others.

Galton was a cousin of Charles Darwin, and was influenced by Darwin's theory of natural selection. Though his work was not particularly well received in Great Britain, it was quickly adopted in the United States. By 1896, Connecticut had already passed a law forbidding marriage between epileptics or the "feeble-minded." As the philosophy spread, those in the "unfit" category included immigrants, minorities, and poor people. African Americans were certainly in that category, but so were Caucasian peoples who were not perceived as society's elite, such as Irish, Polish, and Eastern European ethnicities. Such people were often involuntarily sterilized. Beginning in 1909, the state of California conducted sterilizations on around twenty thousand people in state mental institutions. In 1927, the Supreme Court determined that forced sterilization of the handicapped did not violate the Constitution. (The ruling was overturned in 1942, only after thousands of people had received the procedure.) Thirty-three states allowed involuntary sterilization to be performed on minorities and whomever else lawmakers decided should not be allowed to procreate.

Proponents of eugenics in the early 1900s included cereal magnate John Harvey Kellogg, President Theodore Roosevelt, his Secretary of State Elihu Root, zoologist Charles B. Davenport, Nobel Prize Laureate Hermann J. Muller, and others. National and international organizations were formed, and international conferences were held in 1912, 1921, and 1932. But then Adolph Hitler adopted American eugenics in his goal to create a superior Aryan race. By 1940, hundreds of thousands of Germans with mental or physical disabilities were killed by gas or lethal injection. When Americans saw the horrific things being done, many began to denounce the work of eugenicists. Public opinion had already begun to turn because of religious/moral concerns, although forced sterilizations continued.[62]

The term *eugenics* stopped being used, but the practice has been adapted and fine-tuned under the title of "human genetic engineering" that promises disease prevention or cure, information to warn potential parents of possible undesirable traits in a child, and more. Even so, the process remains controversial. A recent count identified 264 genetics testing companies worldwide that market online and make all kinds of promises.[63]

Some of the social scientists behind creating the questions for standardized IQ tests supported eugenics, so the tests have contained some deep biases at times. Even the SAT exam, developed for college-bound high school students, contains some questions that skew toward some

---

62   "Eugenics," History.com, https://www.history.com/topics/germany/eugenics.

63   Libby Copeland, "You Can Learn a Lot About Yourself from a DNA Test. Here's What Your Genes Cannot Tell You," *Time*, March 2, 2020, https://time.com/5783784/dna-testing-genetics/.

cultures more than others, and can subtly make one group appear more intelligent than another, which is not necessarily the case.

PLESSY V. FERGUSON (1896)

As the tide began to turn against African Americans in the South, the changes were rapid, but not immediate. One of Mark Twain's friends from Hartford, Connecticut, attended an International Exposition in New Orleans in 1885. He wrote that "white and colored people mingled freely, talking and looking at what was of common interest." The two races, he said, associated "in unconscious equality of privileges." Case in point: a Black clergyman was assisting in the service at the most important white Episcopal church in the city.

However, severe changes were looming for African Americans. Historian C. Vann Woodward described the increasing restrictions:

> The first genuine Jim Crow law requiring railroads to carry Negroes in separate cars or behind partitions was adopted by Florida in 1887. Mississippi followed this example in 1888; Texas in 1889; Louisiana in 1890." [The other Southern states quickly followed.]

> Negroes watched with despair while the legal foundations for the Jim Crow system were laid and the walls of segregation mounted around them. Their disenchantment with the hopes based on the Civil War amendments and the Reconstruction laws was nearly complete by 1890. The American commitment to equality, solemnly attested to by three amendments to the Constitution and by elaborate civil rights acts, was virtually repudiated. The "Compromise of 1877" between the Hayes Republicans and the Southern conservatives had resulted in the withdrawal of federal troops from the South and the formal end of Reconstruction. What had started then as a retreat had within a decade turned into a rout. Northern radicals and liberals had abandoned the cause: the courts had rendered the Constitution helpless; the Republican party had forsaken the cause it had sponsored. A tide of racism was mounting in the country unopposed.[64]

---

64 C. Vann Woodward, "Plessy v. Ferguson," *American Heritage*, Vol. 15, Issue 3, 1964, https://www.americanheritage.com/plessy-v-ferguson#1.

Yet in Louisiana in 1890, large numbers of African Americans were still voting, and the Louisiana General Assembly contained sixteen Black senators and representatives, so with the help of Homer A. Plessy pictured right, a decision was made to protest the Jim Crow car bill. They declared it to be "unconstitutional, un-American, unjust, dangerous and against sound public policy." If passed, it promised to be "a free license to the evilly disposed that they might with impunity insult, humiliate, and otherwise maltreat inoffensive persons, especially women and children who would happen to have a dark skin."

The arrest of Homer A. Plessy and subsequent court case, Plessy v. Ferguson, led to the "separate but equal" doctrine which remained legally enforceable until 1954.

Still, the bill was passed, so the protesting group determined to challenge the whites-only railroad cars with a test case. As it turned out, they discovered they could work with the railroads they were protesting. Louisiana railroad officials had already determined the law was "a bad and mean one" they would like to get rid of, and had told conductors to post the required sign but not bother anyone who ignored the instruction. For them, providing separate whites-only cars was an unnecessary additional expense.

Homer Adolph Plessy was selected to challenge the injustices that were being instituted. He was, by his own definition, "seven-eighths Caucasian and one-eighth African blood" and would later testify in court that "the admixture of colored blood is not discernible." He bought a ticket for a destination within Louisiana (to avoid any potential interstate complications) and sat down in the whites-only car. Since Plessy could easily pass for white, it was assumed that the railroad had been informed of the plan and was willing to cooperate. [65]

Plessy was escorted off the train by a police detective and later went to court. He filed a petition against his presiding judge, John Ferguson, asserting that the railroad car bill violated the equal protection clause of the Fourteenth Amendment. His case eventually ended up before the Supreme Court. On May 18, 1896, the Court deemed that the "separate but equal" doctrine was constitutional. However, they ruled that the Fourteenth Amendment applied only to political and civil rights (voting, jury service, and so forth), not "social rights" such as sitting in the railroad car of your choice.

The lone dissenting voice, again, was Justice John Marshall Harlan. He argued: "The arbitrary separation of citizens on the basis of race while they are on a public highway is a badge of servitude wholly inconsistent with the civil freedom and the equality before the law established by the Constitution. It cannot be justified upon any legal grounds."[66]

"Separate but equal" may have sounded good and reasonable in theory: Black people would be provided the same rights and privileges as whites, but the two groups would not mix. In practicality, however, the doctrine worked in separating Blacks from whites as can be seen in the photos to the right, but it never provided equality.

65   Ibid.

66   "Plessy v. Ferguson," History.com, https://www.history.com/topics/black-history/plessy-v-ferguson.

In practicality, the doctrine of "separate but equal" worked in separating Blacks from whites, but it never provided equality.

Segregation became the law of the land, spreading to hotels, restaurants, theaters, and even schools. The "separate but equal" way of operating continued until another Supreme Court case in 1954: *Brown v. Board of Education*, when the majority of the Justices would essentially agree (at last) with Harlan's minority opinion in *Plessy v. Ferguson*.

Plessy attempted a great service to a community of African American people because he felt connectivity with them, even though he could have lived a much more carefree and privileged life if he just passed as somebody white. Yet he was committed to trying to bring about justice and righteousness.

Instead of striving for racial equality, Booker T. Washington encouraged African Americans to get educated or learn trades that would provide them with a decent living.

THE "ATLANTA COMPROMISE" (1895)

Booker T. Washington, pictured addressing a crowd above, was the most influential spokesman for Black Americans between 1895 and his death in 1915. Although born in slave quarters, his commitment to education after emancipation led to his being named to oversee the school that would become Tuskegee University. As he witnessed the ongoing struggles African Americans were having to endure, despite the promising improvements that had been witnessed during Reconstruction, he sensed that his people might be reaching for too much, too soon.

In a historic speech that came to be known as the "Atlanta Compromise," Washington noted that people of color comprised a third of the population of the South, most of them poor and illiterate laborers who were never going to be high-level politicians or social figures. Rather than encouraging them to keep striving so hard for civil rights and social equality, he instead recommended they devote themselves to productive work in agriculture, mechanics, commerce, domestic service, and similar professions. Here are a few of the key points from his speech:[67]

> » "No race can prosper till it learns that there is as much dignity in tilling a field as in writing a poem. It is at the bottom of life we must begin, and not at the top. Nor should we permit our grievances to overshadow our opportunities."
> » "In all things that are purely social we can be as separate as the fingers, yet one as the hand in all things essential to mutual progress."
> » "The opportunity to earn a dollar in a factory just now is worth infinitely more than the opportunity to spend a dollar in an opera-house."

Washington's suggested "compromise" was that the dominant white South allow Blacks to be educated and learn trades that would provide them a decent living. In time, they would earn the acceptance of the white community and, eventually, equality. But in the meantime, they would give up their demands to have all the rights and privileges of whites, even if it meant willingly enduring prejudice and discrimination.

Washington's speech was well received by whites in both the North and South, and by many African Americans as well—but not so much by educated Blacks.

THE NIAGARA MOVEMENT (1905) AND THE NAACP (1909)

One of Booker T. Washington's most outspoken critics was W. E. B. Du Bois, a noted historian and Black protest leader who did not care for Washington's "accommodation" philosophy. He responded to Washington in a book published in 1903:

It has been claimed that the Negro can survive only through submission. Mr. Washington distinctly asks that Black people give up, at least for the present, three things,—

---

67   Louis R. Harlan, ed., *The Booker T. Washington Papers*, Vol. 3 (Urbana: University of Illinois Press, 1974), pp. 583-587, cited in "Booker T. Washington Delivers the 1895 Atlanta Compromise Speech" History Matters, http://historymatters.gmu.edu/d/39/.

First, political power,
Second, insistence on civil rights,
Third, higher education of Negro youth,

—and concentrate all their energies on industrial education, the accu-
mulation of wealth, and the conciliation of the South. This policy has
been courageously and insistently advocated for over fifteen years, and
has been triumphant for perhaps ten years. As a result of this tender
of the palm-branch, what has been the return? In these years there
have occurred:

1) The disfranchisement of the Negro.
2) The legal creation of a distinct status of civil inferiority for the Negro.
3) The steady withdrawal of aid from institutions for the higher
training of the Negro.

These movements are not, to be sure, direct results of Mr. Washington's teachings; but his propaganda has, without a shadow of doubt,
helped their speedier accomplishment.[68]

Du Bois was growing more determined than ever that Washington's strategy would only solidify the oppressive conditions of
Blacks. Change, he was convinced, would only occur through protest and active resistance. His convictions led to the establishment of

Niagara Movement

68   W. E. Burghardt Du Bois, *The Souls of Black Folk* (Chicago, 1903), cited in "W.E.B. Du Bois
Critiques Booker T. Washington," History Matters, http://historymatters.gmu.edu/d/40.

Ida Wells–Barett   *W. E. B. Du Bois*   *Henry Moscowitz*

Mary White   *Oswald*   *William*
Ovington   *Garrison Villiard*   *English Walling*

the Niagara Movement. Du Bois and a small group of like-minded African Americans, shown on the facing page, gathered at Niagara Falls to brainstorm. (They had to meet on the Canadian side when no US hotel would admit them.)

The group compiled a list of demands, including an end to segregation, equal opportunity for economic and educational advancement, and no more discrimination in courts or public facilities. They had no authority to enforce any of their desires, and their effect on legislation was negligible.

However, four years later some race riots in Illinois captured the attention of some notable white progressives, including Jane Addams and John Dewey. In response, they founded the National Association for the Advancement of Colored People (NAACP), using many of the objectives of the Niagara Movement as their goals. They even hired W. E. B. Du Bois to direct publicity and research, and to edit their journal.[69] From its beginning, as seen above, the NAACP was a

---

69   "Niagara Movement," History.com, https://www.history.com/topics/black-history/niagara-movement.

mix of Black and white individuals working together to address the issues concerning the advancement of Black people.

As African American leaders saw their freedoms rapidly declining, they struggled to devise a strategy that would sustain equality for Blacks and whites. But no reasonable answers were to be found because the Southern attitude toward people of color was unreasonable. Booker T. Washington's proposed compromise was not the solution. W. E. B. Du Bois's plan of resistance was unenforceable. It appeared there was no way to stop the return of the oppression they had struggled so long to overcome. To make things worse, events in the first half of the twentieth century would cripple them both socially and economically. The lives of Black Americans—especially those in the South—were going to get much worse before they got better.

Why are we still off-base about race? As we have seen, the equitable resolution of any problem requires the efforts of both (or all) parties involved. In matters involving racial division in America, this has rarely been the case. One group suggests compromise; the other demands concession. One demands justice but lacks the power to enforce it; the other ignores the issue, lacking the empathy and mercy to care. Until both sides agree to work together to resolve the root issues of race, conflicts are likely to continue.

7

Institutionalized Separation
(History: 1910–1950)

The Reconstruction Era looked like it might be a long-deserved turning point for the treatment and status of Black people in the United States. At long last, African Americans had a constitutional right to claim citizenship, to vote, and to buy and sell property. Former slaves stepped into leadership roles and proved to be among the greatest minds of that period of history. But as soon as the protective federal troops were removed from the South, the numbers of their antagonistic white adversaries were just too great to overcome. Constitutional guarantees were short-circuited by locally imposed Black codes and Jim Crow laws, which were immorally and illegally enforced not only by biased elected law enforcement officers, but also by the covert and insidious activity of the Ku Klux Klan.

This chapter will provide several examples to demonstrate two primary methods used by racist crowds to prevent African Americans from achieving any semblance of equality with whites: fear and economic discrimination.

BIRTH OF A NATION

In 1915, a movie was released called *Birth of a Nation*. It has been hailed as a great work of innovative movie-making, but it also has a well-deserved reputation as one of the most offensive films ever made. Based on a book titled *The Clansman*, the movie presented an extremely one-sided and twisted history of the Reconstruction Era following the Civil War. The freed slaves were portrayed as essentially useless for anything except subservient labor, and they were easily manipulated by radical Republicans to intimidate Southern whites. Some scenes showed Black men running around like animals and raping white women.

In contrast, Ku Klux Klan members were presented as heroes who fought against not only the Northern overseers and Southern Blacks who threatened their way of life but also immigrants, Jews, and Roman Catholics. A reviewer in *The New Yorker* wrote of the movie's "disgusting content" and how it "proved horrifically effective at sparking violence against blacks in many cities," yet had to paradoxically admit, "The worst thing about 'Birth of a Nation' is how good it is."[70] The movie remained a controversial source of contention throughout much of the 1900s. The NAACP picketed outside theaters and attempted (often unsuccessfully) to prevent its showing, while the Klan used it to recruit members. In the 1920s, Klan membership exceeded four million people nationwide.[71]

The gross misrepresentations in this movie—both the depravity of Black men and the heroism of the KKK—may have fueled much of the hatred toward people of color that was so rampant in the South during the 1900s.

LYNCHING

Lynching involves taking the law into one's own hands and passing judgment—usually a death sentence—on a victim for an offense without benefit of a trial. Lynching was frequently done by unruly

70   Richard Brody, "The Worst Thing about 'Birth of a Nation' Is How Good It Is," *The New Yorker*, Feb. 1, 2013, https://www.newyorker.com/culture/richard-brody/the-worst-thing-about-birth-of-a-nation-is-how-good-it-is.

71   "Ku Klux Klan," History.com, https://www.history.com/topics/reconstruction/ku-klux-klan.

mobs who imposed sadistic torture. The accused's "offenses" were often contrived, and the person had no opportunity to present a defense.

Lynching had been around since Colonial America; eighteen enslaved Blacks who had planned an escape were manacled, burned, and broken on the wheel in New York City in 1712. But lynching became much more public and prominent beginning in 1877, after the Tilden-Hayes compromise that ended Reconstruction in the South. Lynchings had little to do with justice. Most historians agree they were a means of social and racial control intended to force Black people into submission and an acceptance of an inferior status through the use of terror.[72]

People of color had little recourse when confronted by a lynch mob. The criminal charges did not have to be true. Legal representation was seldom an option. When word of a lynching started to spread, not only would officers often leave the victim's cell unguarded and available to the mob, but also those very officers would often be participants in the lynching. The methods of killing were horrific. Hanging was common, but sometimes bodies were also burned and mutilated.

W. E. B. Du Bois wrote about many of the gruesome details of lynching in his autobiography:

> In the autobiographical writings, Du Bois underscores a ghastly incident that shook him to his core during this period—the lynching of Sam Hose in April 1899. Hose was a farmer in Palmetto, Georgia, a few miles outside Atlanta, who had shot and killed a white farmer after an argument over a debt. Accounts differ as to whether he raped the wife as her dead husband lay nearby on the kitchen floor. Justice was summary, ghoulish. After lynching and burning Hose to death, the white mob of two thousand men, women, and children had fought over pieces of his flesh for souvenirs.[73]

---

72   Jamiles Lartey and Sam Morris, "How White Americans Used Lynchings to Terrorize and Control Black People," *The Guardian*, April 26, 2018, https://www.theguardian.com/us-news/2018/apr/26/lynchings-memorial-us-south-montgomery-alabama.

73   David Levering Lewis, *W.E.B. Du Bois: A Biography* (New York: Henry Holt and Company, 2009), p. 162.

Du Bois went on to describe how the knuckles of the victim were put on display at a local store and that the state's governor had been presented with a piece of the man's heart and liver.

One particularly disturbing aspect of lynchings was that there was no public outrage over such atrocities. A North Carolina paper wrote: "Whole families came together, mothers and fathers, bringing even their youngest children. It was the show of the countryside—a very popular show. Men joked loudly at the sight of the bleeding body. . . . Girls giggled as the flies fed on the blood that dripped from the Negro's nose." And a Missouri paper noted that approximately 2,000 to 4,000 people attended the lynching, and it was comprised of at least one-fourth women and hundreds of children. One woman "held her little girl up so she could get a better view of the naked Negro blazing on the roof."[74]

Women were not spared the rage of lynch mobs. In Georgia in 1918, a white farmer named Hampton Smith was murdered. Smith had the habit of bailing Black people out of jail after they had been accused of some petty crime, and then having them work at his farm to pay off the debt. He was known to be an abusive employer, which one day led to an argument with a worker named Sidney Johnson who ended up killing Smith. Johnson confessed to the killing, but he was killed by police in a shootout. And even though they had a confession, the white community decided to level a charge of conspiracy against several other Black farm workers who had been associated with Smith. They lynched at least seven of them. One of their victims was a man named Hayes Turner.

The next day Turner's wife, Mary, in her grief, threatened legal action. It was an empty threat because Black people had no voice in the Southern legal system at that time. But Mary's threat was enough to agitate the white community. A mob took her, tied her up, and hanged

---

74   Jamiles Lartey and Sam Morris, "How White Americans Used Lynchings to Terrorize and Control Black People," *The Guardian*, April 26, 2018 https://www.theguardian.com/us-news/2018/apr/26/lynchings-memorial-us-south-montgomery-alabama.

her by her feet from a tree. They threw gasoline on her and burned her clothes off. She was eight months pregnant, and they used a butcher's knife to cut the baby from her body. When it fell to the ground, it was reported that the assembled crowd stomped on it. Then they made sure Mary was dead by shooting her hundreds of times as she hung there ... all for speaking out against the lynching of her husband.[75]

While Black people were often lynched without just or probable cause, white people were sometimes lynched simply because they were standing up for the Black victim. One notable example occurred during the Omaha race riot of 1919. Racial tension in the country was high. Fifty-four Blacks had been lynched in the United States by 1916, and in many cities like Omaha, politicians had established strongholds by exaggerating the threat that had been portrayed in *Birth of a Nation*—Black men preying on white women. This spreading fear had not only kept aggressive white leaders in power, but was also used to legitimize many sex-related lynchings of African Americans. Omaha had a strong political boss named Tom Dennison in place but had elected a white mayor, Edward P. Smith, who was promoting reform.

The catalyst for the conflict in Omaha was the accusation of assault by a white couple, Milton Hoffman and Agnes Loeback. They said that Hoffman had been robbed, and nineteen-year-old Loeback had been raped. The next day's newspaper headline reported a "black beast" who had assaulted a white girl. Meanwhile, Agnes's brother had organized a group of four hundred armed men (including many railroad workers who knew Alice) to search out the assailant. When they heard a neighbor report a "suspicious negro," that's all it took. Will Brown was accused of raping a white woman and given no opportunity to respond to the charge.[76]

---

75   "Mary Turner, Pregnant, Lynched in Georgia for Publicly Criticizing Husband's Lynching," *Equal Justice Initiative*, https://calendar.eji.org/racial-injustice/may/19.

76   "Lest we Forget: The Lynching of Will Brown, Omaha's 1919 Race Riot," History Nebraska Blog, Accessed Nov. 17, 2020 https://history.nebraska.gov/blog/lest-we-forget-lynching-will-brown-omaha%E2%80%99s-1919-race-riot.

The next day a crowd began to gather around the Douglas County courthouse where Brown was being held. As the day passed, an estimated crowd of 5,000 to 15,000 gathered outside, growing more agitated. By 8 p.m., they began to shoot into the courthouse with guns from nearby stores they had looted. Two people were killed. By 8:30 they had broken out windows on the lower floors, set the building on fire, and would not allow firemen access to put out the flames. The Omaha police and city officials were essentially prisoners. Mayor Smith, pictured below, who had been present for hours, went out to confront the mob, asking it to allow firemen to extinguish the flames.[77] A first-person account describes what happened next:

> Mayor Ed Smith came out the east doors on Seventeenth Street to confront the mob, calling upon them to let the law take its course. His appeal was short-lived. He was hit with a baseball bat or other blunt object (Leonard Weber later said he hit the mayor over the head with a gun.) and received a dozen other blows. "No, I will not give up the man," Smith said. "I'm going to enforce the law even with my own life." The crowd took his words to heart, shouting "hang him" and "string him up." With a noose around his neck, the mayor was dragged along Harney Street to the Sixteenth Street traffic signal tower. The rope was thrown over a bar and tightened around Smith's neck when Russell Norgaard saved the mayor's life by removing the rope. (Emmett C. Hoctor wrote in a letter that a witness, requesting anonymity, identified his uncle, James P. Hoctor, as the man who removed the rope from Smith's neck.)[78]

Omaha mayor, Ed Smith, narrowly escaped with his life when he refused to surrender Will Brown to the mob.

77 "A Horrible Lynching," net: Nebraska's PBS & NPR Stations, Accessed Nov. 17, 2020, http://www.nebraskastudies.org/en/1900-1924/racial-tensions/a-horrible-lynching/.

78 Letter to Emmett C. Hoctor from anonymous, Omaha, Nebraska, May 25, 1919. Copy in possession of Orville D. Menard. https://history.nebraska.gov/sites/history.nebraska.gov/files/

Despite Mayor Smith's efforts, the enraged mob—as can be seen below—finally got to Will Brown. He was beaten into unconsciousness, dragged to a nearby lamp pole, hanged, riddled with bullets, brought down and tied behind a car, towed to another intersection

Bystanders grin as Will Brown's body is burned during his lynching on September 28, 1919, in Omaha, Nebraska.

where his body was doused with lamp fuel and burned, and then dragged through the streets of downtown Omaha.[79]

Of all the horrendous and evil events connected with this event, perhaps the worst is that it may have been motivated more by political opportunity than genuine racial hatred. According to one report, "Political boss Tom Dennison and his allies may have encouraged the lynching in order to discredit Mayor Edward P. Smith, an advocate for reform. . . . Brown may have been the victim of a politically

doc/publications/NH2010Lynching.pdf .

79   "A Horrible Lynching . . ."

inspired maneuver to restore the city officials dislodged by the 1918 election. Brown's death was timely, if not timed, to provide an opportunity to strike hard at Mayor Ed Smith. Dennison's machine won the next election."[80]

It is distressing to repeat in such graphic detail what was taking place during this phase of American history, but if we attempt to minimize or overlook the senselessness and violence, we miss the point. I do want to emphasize that while lynching was a prominent method used by some whites to control Blacks, other whites found it repulsive. Mayor Smith was just one example. As we think of those who were wrongfully and needlessly abused and killed in the effort to establish more equality between the races, we need to acknowledge the whites who suffered and died as well as the many Black victims. More of them will be highlighted as we continue our look at history.

Lynchings went on for decades, well into the 1960s. Some people argue that if we use the literal definition for lynching, the term applies to the death of George Floyd in Minneapolis on May 25, 2020. On that day: (1) a crowd was present, including law enforcement officers; (2) Floyd was afforded no due process of law; and (3) his life was terminated.

Not surprisingly, Black communities still hold strong suspicions about law enforcement officers because, historically, the law was frequently used to enforce segregation. Such suspicions are understandable, especially in light of recent statistics that show how Blacks continue to be stopped and searched by officers much more frequently than whites. Encounters with police can incite fear and/or panic. Yet I would encourage us to remember that many white officers, on behalf of Black people, put their lives on the line every day. They are injured and sometimes killed because they are committed to serve and protect *all* communities—Black and white. May God

---

80   "Lest We Forget: . . ."

help us to begin to see beyond a person's skin color and intensify our efforts to live as one race—the human race.

Archives at the Tuskegee Institute have listed 4,743 people who died at the hands of US lynch mobs between 1881 and 1968. Nearly three-fourths of them were Black.[81] Many others were from non-white nationalities or cultures. Most states report lynchings at some point in their history, and it is believed that the actual number has been vastly underreported. They were more prominent in the South, although the Equal Justice Initiative (EJI) has recently documented an abundance of these violent acts in Illinois, Indiana, Kansas, Maryland, Missouri, Ohio, Oklahoma, and West Virginia. At the end of a comprehensive report based on six years of meticulous research into lynching in America, the EJI concludes:

> Lynching in America was a form of terrorism that has contributed to a legacy of racial inequality that our nation must address more directly and concretely than we have to date. The trauma and anguish that lynching and racial violence created in this country continues to haunt us and to contaminate race relations and our criminal justice system in too many places across this country. Important work can and must be done to speak truthfully about this difficult history so that recovery and reconciliation can be achieved. We can address our painful past by acknowledging it and embracing monuments, memorials, and markers that are designed to facilitate important conversations. Education must be accompanied by acts of reconciliation, which are needed to create communities where devastating acts of racial bigotry and legacies of racial injustice can be overcome. [82]

TULSA RACE MASSACRE OF 1921

Prejudice-based violence was not confined to lynchings, nor to the Southeast. One often overlooked success story for freed slaves during Reconstruction was in Tulsa, Oklahoma, but it was followed by one of the cruelest massacres in our nation's history.

---

81   Lartay and Morris, "How White Americans . . ."

82   "Lynching in America: Confronting the Legacy of Racial Terror," *Equal Justice Initiative*, 2017, https://lynchinginamerica.eji.org/report/.

After the Civil War, Oklahoma became a safer place for African Americans than their former homes in the Southeast. By 1920, more than fifty Black towns had been founded there. Some of the Native Americans who had been forcibly relocated to Oklahoma had owned slaves who remained in the area and continued to live on reservation land. Many other sharecroppers relocated there to escape the racial oppression of the Southern states.

A wealthy Black man named O. W. Gurley bought forty acres of land in Tulsa with "a vision to create something for black people by black people." He opened a boarding house that welcomed African Americans and offered loans to Black people who wanted to open a business. A community began to form, which he named Greenwood after a town in Mississippi. Tulsa was a strictly segregated city, so African Americans naturally gathered in Greenwood. A publisher started a Black newspaper that kept the community aware of its rights and opportunities. A lawyer moved in and opened a luxury hotel—the largest Black-owned hotel in the nation.

As word spread, Greenwood soon became a self-contained community with stores, restaurants, movie theaters, groceries, nightclubs, barbershops, and hair salons. It had its own school system, post office, library, hospital, bus service, and savings and loan. Doctors, dentists, and lawyers set up offices. It was an economically mixed community. Many earned a living outside of Greenwood as house cleaners, janitors, or other low-level positions. Others, however, lived in large houses with nice furniture, fine china, crystal, and such.

However, the success, visibility, and economic stability of Greenwood evoked jealousy and resentment in racist Oklahoma. Across the nation in 1919, anti-Black riots and lynchings had been taking place, including in Tulsa. The Black newspaper had encouraged residents of Greenwood to arm themselves and position themselves at jails and trials of Blacks to ensure their sentences were not preempted by a lynch mob.[83]

But the racial tension did not subside. Two years later Tulsa was the scene of one of the most horrific race riots in history. The Tulsa Historical Society describes the events:

Following World War I, Tulsa was recognized nationally for its affluent African American community known as the Greenwood District. This thriving business district and surrounding residential area was referred to as "Black Wall Street." In June 1921, a series of events nearly destroyed the entire Greenwood area.

On the morning of May 30, 1921, a young black man named Dick Rowland was riding in the elevator in the Drexel Building at Third and Main with a white woman named Sarah Page. The details of what followed vary from person to person. Accounts of an incident circulated among the city's white community during the day and became more exaggerated with each telling.

Tulsa police arrested Rowland the following day and began an investigation. An inflammatory report in the May 31 edition of the Tulsa *Tribune* spurred a confrontation between black and white armed mobs around the courthouse where the sheriff and his men had barricaded the top floor to protect Rowland. Shots were fired, and the outnumbered African Americans began retreating to the Greenwood District.

In the early morning hours of June 1, 1921, Greenwood was looted and burned by white rioters. Governor Robertson declared martial law, and National Guard troops arrived in Tulsa. Guardsmen assisted firemen in putting out fires, took African Americans out of the hands of vigilantes and imprisoned all black Tulsans not already interned. Over 6,000 people were held at the Convention Hall and the Fairgrounds, some for as long as eight days.

Twenty-four hours after the violence erupted, it ceased. In the wake of the violence, 35 city blocks lay in charred ruins, more than 800 people

83   Alexis Clark, "Tulsa's 'Black Wall Street' Flourished as a Self-Contained Hub in Early 1900s," History.com, Jan 2, 2020, https://www.history.com/news/black-wall-street-tulsa-race-massacre.

were treated for injuries and contemporary reports of deaths began at 36. Historians now believe as many as 300 people may have died.[84]

Walter White, the assistant secretary of the NAACP, went to Tulsa to see the aftermath of the riot and described it in a magazine article, portions of which were used in the Introduction of a book about the massacre. He describes Tulsa as a city that was on edge to begin with:

> What are the causes of the race riot that occurred in such a place? First, the Negro in Oklahoma has shared in the sudden prosperity that has come to many of his white brothers, and there are some colored men there who are wealthy. This fact has caused a bitter resentment on the part of the lower order of whites, who feel that these colored men, members of an "inferior race," are exceedingly presumptuous in achieving greater economic prosperity than they who are members of a divinely ordered superior race. . . .

> One of the charges made against the colored men in Tulsa is that they were "radical." Questioning the whites more closely regarding the nature of this radicalism, I found it means that Negroes were uncompromisingly denouncing "Jim-Crow" [railroad] cars, lynching, peonage; in short, were asking that the Federal constitutional guaranties of "life, liberty, and the pursuit of happiness" be given regardless of color. . . .

> A third cause was the rotten political conditions in Tulsa. A vice ring was in control of the city, allowing open operation of houses of ill fame, of gambling joints, the illegal sale of whiskey, the robbing of banks and stores, with hardly a slight possibility of the arrest of the criminals, and even less of their conviction. . . .

In the article, White described Sarah Page as "a hysterical white girl." As for the charges against Dick Rowland, he added:

> It was found afterwards that the boy had stepped by accident on her foot. It seems never to have occurred to the citizens of Tulsa that any

---

84 "1921 Tulsa Race Massacre," *Tulsa Historical Society and Museum*, https://www.tulsahistory.org/exhibit/1921-tulsa-race-massacre/#flexible-content.

sane person attempting criminally to assault a woman would have picked any place in the world other than an open elevator in a public building with scores of people within calling distance.[85]

The Tulsa Historical Society summarizes:

In order to understand the Tulsa Race Massacre it is important to understand the complexities of the times. Dick Rowland, Sarah Page and an unknown gunman were the sparks that ignited a long smoldering fire. Jim Crow, jealousy, white supremacy, and land lust, all played roles in leading up to the destruction and loss of life on May 31 and June 1, 1921.[86]

Race is an important subject that we need to treat with dignity. I hope that by now you can see why we need a deeper understanding of its historic roots. We cannot start by asking, "What do we do to solve it?" First we need to address the deeper issue of "How did we get here?" If we want to uproot the disease, it starts by diagnosing the problem to create a new prognosis. The very first thing we need to do is really understand the pathology of this disease, so we have been spending time in history and the trajectory of what happened with slavery and subsequent injustices against Black people.

ECONOMIC INEQUITY

We have seen some of the awful consequences of prejudice expressed by individuals, groups of individuals, and even state and local governments. While white supremacist groups were using violence to persecute African Americans throughout the nation during the first half of the twentieth century, the federal government was beginning to make life for Black people harder than it should have been by oppressing them financially.

In 1934, the Federal Housing Administration (FHA) and the Department of Veterans Affairs (VA) were very much involved in

---

85   Walter White, "The Eruption of Tulsa," *Nation*, June 29, 1921, cited in Introduction of Hannibal B. Johnson, *Black Wall Street 100* (Fort Worth: Eakin Press, 2020).

86   "1921 Tulsa Race Massacre," Ibid.

segregating communities. They used a method that came to be known as *redlining*: Lenders used red ink to outline on maps the sections of a city that they considered high risks for default. Redlined areas were predominantly Black and Latino. The federal government created these maps in conjunction with local real estate agents in cities with populations of forty thousand or more—especially those with a large percentage of minorities—including Chicago, Detroit, Tampa, and Atlanta.

The result was that builders did not construct new homes in Black communities because the federal government would not insure loans there. Even when buyers had excellent credit, banks and lenders would reject their loans just because of their race or where they lived.[87]

After WWII, the VA adopted similar procedures. The housing market was flooded with homes in certain neighborhoods available for purchase with a low down payment and interest rates as low as 3 percent, but African Americans were refused those special loans. If they wanted to live in those neighborhoods, they would have needed perhaps 20 percent down to purchase that home. So even when African Americans began making the same amount of money that whites were making, they still were not entitled to the same privileges. Although redlining was prohibited after the 1968 Fair Housing Act and the 1977 Community Reinvestment Act, the discriminatory consequences of this practice are still evident in many US communities today.

Another discriminatory housing example after World War II—an even more overt one—was what was known as Levittown. A developer named William J. Levitt devised a way to mass produce new homes in as little as a day. He would create large suburban housing developments and market homes to qualified veterans at much less

---

87   Khristopher J. Brooks, "Redlining's Legacy: Maps Are Gone, but the Problem Hasn't Disappeared," CBS News, June 12, 2020, https://www.cbsnews.com/news/redlining-what-is-history-mike-bloomberg-comments/.

than they would pay to rent. The typical home would include modern appliances, green lawns, and white picket fences.

> Levittown was a massive undertaking, a development of 17,500 homes. It was a visionary solution to the housing problems of returning war veterans—mass-produced two-bedroom houses of 750 square feet sold for about $8,000 each, with no down payment required. William Levitt constructed the project on speculation; it was not a case in which prospective purchasers gave the company funds with which to construct houses. Instead, Levitt built the houses and then sought customers. He could never have amassed the capital for such an enormous undertaking without the FHA and the VA. But during the World War II years and after, the government had congressional authority to guarantee bank loans to mass-production builders like Levitt for nearly the full cost of their proposed subdivisions. By 1948, most housing nationwide was being constructed with this government financing.[88]

It sounded like a great deal for returning soldiers, right? There was just one drawback: Each deed contained a legal covenant that prohibited Blacks from living there. Home buyers had to sign that covenant before they moved into the outwardly segregated community of Levittown.

One of the men instrumental in building the first Levittown was an African American named Robert Mereday. He had started his own business using repurposed, inexpensive Army surplus trucks to haul heavy loads. Levitt had hired him to haul cement blocks that lined the community's cesspools, and later gave him a contract to deliver drywall. Mereday soon had a small fleet of trucks driven by several of his nephews who had returned from military service. He was a responsible business owner raising a family on a respectable middle-class income. He was as qualified as anyone else who was buying the Levittown homes, but he did not even try. He told his son, "It was generally known that black people couldn't buy into the

---

88   Richard Rothstein, *The Color of Law: A Forgotten History of How Our Government Segregated America* (New York: Liveright Publishing, 2017), pp. 70-71.

development. When you grow up and live in a place, you know what the rules are."[89]

One of Robert Mereday's nephews tried to buy one of the homes but was turned down. He was a Navy veteran who had also been turned down for flight training because of his color, and had only been allowed to serve as a mechanic. Instead of a Levittown home with no down payment and a low interest mortgage, he had to buy a house in a neighboring, almost all-Black suburb with a substantial down payment and an uninsured mortgage with high interest rates. He was "permanently embittered" by the discrimination he had experienced in the Navy and the real estate market.[90]

Still, the first Levittown in New York was such a success that others followed in Pennsylvania, New Jersey, Maryland, and Puerto Rico.

But what does this really mean? What is the real effect of having to pay a little more for a home? It means the white residents of a Levittown community could acquire one of those $8,000 homes with no down payment and a low mortgage rate. In time, the housing market exploded and the price of those homes shot up in value. Some of those very same homes today sell for between $300,000 and $400,000. Minorities who were blocked from such government-guaranteed deals had to settle for lesser homes (if they could afford a 20 percent down payment) and then struggle to meet the monthly payments with the high interest rates. The difference could mean sending your kids to college, or not. Eating healthy meals, or not. Being able to transfer wealth to the next generation, or not. It has been estimated that Black families whose homes were redlined forty years ago have lost out on at least $212,000 in personal wealth during that time span. Redlining is one of the primary reasons for the significant gap

---

89   Ibid. pp. 68-69.

90   Ibid. p. 69.

in wealth between Blacks and whites today.[91] And it was all done with the full knowledge and approval of the United States government.

And there are other consequences for minorities because of those housing injustices. By stacking the decks to give whites privileges the Blacks did not have, it influenced the whole perception of competence and intelligence. The differences were not attributed to an unjust exclusion of privilege by the federal government, but rather a genetic difference. People began to perceive, wrongly, that whites were better financial managers than Blacks. They appeared to have more right to prosper. Blacks began to be viewed as a little less intelligent, a little less moral, a little less mindful, a little less responsible.

WIDESPREAD PREJUDICE

In the early 1900s, certain locations throughout the country came to be known as "sundown towns"—all-white communities that discouraged Black residents by using threats, intimidation, and violence if necessary. By necessity, African Americans would need to travel through these towns at times, but they knew not to linger, and they were warned not to be there after dark. Many cities had signs posted. One Arkansas town boasted, "Cool Summers, Mild Winters, No Blizzards, No Negroes." Many read, "Whites Only After Dark." On some, the message was stronger, addressing Black travelers with a most defamatory racist term and the warning, "Don't Let the Sun Go Down on You in This Town." Some of these signs were seen as recently as the 1970s.

Even during the daytime, African Americans in sundown towns would frequently face threats or even beatings and/or arrests. Often law enforcement officers would follow Black drivers to the city limits. Occasionally Black travelers were lynched.

By 1930, half of the counties along Route 66, the main passage from Chicago to Los Angeles, prohibited Blacks from after-dark

---

91   Khristopher Brooks, "Redlining's Legacy . . ."

stops at restaurants or motels. Such widespread, constant potential danger to Black travelers led to the creation and publication of the *Negro Motorist Green Book*, more commonly referred to as simply the green book. Victor Green, a Harlem postal worker, compiled a list of places throughout the country for African Americans to safely stay overnight, eat out, get their cars serviced, and so forth. Published between 1936 and 1966, at one point the green book was being used by two million people.[92]

If you have never heard of sundown towns, do not feel too bad. You are not the only one. Author James Loewen explains:

> Even though sundown towns were everywhere, almost no literature exists on the topic. No book has ever been written about the making of all-white towns in America. Indeed, this story is so unknown as to deserve the term *hidden*. Most Americans have no idea such towns or counties exist, or they think such things happened mainly in the Deep South. Ironically, the traditional South has almost no sundown towns. Mississippi, for instance, has no more than six, mostly mere hamlets, while Illinois has no fewer than 456. . . .
>
> Even book-length studies of individual sundown towns rarely mention their exclusionary policies. Local historians omit the fact intentionally, knowing that it would reflect badly on their communities if publicized abroad. I read at least 300 local histories—some of them elaborate coffee-table books—about towns whose sundown histories I had confirmed via detailed oral histories, but only about 1 percent of these mentioned their town's racial policies. In conversation, however, the authors of these commemorative histories were often more forthcoming, showing that they knew about the policy but didn't care to disclose it in print.[93]

When you really start to look at how severely African Americans were oppressed during this era of history, it is no surprise that issues

---

92   Ross Coen, "Sundown Towns," *BlackPast*, August 23, 2020, https://www.blackpast.org/african-american-history/sundown-towns/.

93   James W. Loewen, *Sundown Towns: A Hidden Dimension of American Racism* (New York: The New Press, 2005), p. 5.

of racism continue to plague our nation. Slavery as an institution had been outlawed, but that had done little to change Black/white relationships on a national level. How could such an unjust system ever be changed? We will look at that in the next chapter.

Why are we still off-base about race? As we have seen in this chapter, the roots of racial strife grow deep into the most cruel, depraved, and merciless aspects of humanity. When oppressors become so violent, so heartless, and so desensitized to the pain they are inflicting . . . when the government actively discriminates against a large segment of American citizens to prevent them from becoming economically stable . . . when constitutional rights are not only ignored, but intentionally and repeatedly violated . . . how can the result be anything but lasting rage and resentment?

8

Heroes and Martyrs
(History: 1950–1965)

Children are influenced very early in life by images they see in the world around them. The bombardment of news, media, peers, and family all affect the way they see the world and one another. By the mid-1900s, generations of Black children had been brought up in a culture claiming to be "separate but equal" when it came to Blacks and whites. (You may remember the 1896 *Plessy v. Ferguson* ruling from the previous chapter.) But did the children believe that was true?

In the 1940s, an African American couple named Clark, both holding doctorates in psychology, conducted a series of experiments known as the Doll Test. They interviewed 253 Black children between the ages of three and seven and showed each child four dolls. Two dolls had brown skin and black hair; the other two had white skin and yellow hair.[94]

Then they asked the child to answer some questions: Which doll would you rather play with? Which ones are nice? Which ones are bad? Which one is most like you? The participants overwhelmingly preferred the white dolls to the black dolls, and even identified the

94   Leila McNeill, "How a Psychologist's Work on Race Identity Helped Overturn School Segregation in 1950s America," *Smithsonian Magazine*, Oct. 26, 2017, https://www.smithsonianmag.com/science-nature/psychologist-work-racial-identity-helped-overturn-school-segregation-180966934/.

white dolls as looking most like them. Even by that age, the kids had already internalized that there was something bad about being Black and something good about being white. The results proved to the Clarks that forced segregation created a lifelong sense of inferiority in children.[95]

Studies that replicated the Doll Test were conducted in 2005 and 2010. You would think that by then Black children would have developed a better self-image, but that didn't appear to be the case. You can see segments of both experiments on YouTube.[96]

BROWN V. BOARD OF EDUCATION (1954)

In the early 1950s, the NAACP was actively opposing segregation by bringing lawsuits against schools. Lead counsel at the time was Thurgood Marshall—in the middle in the picture to the right—and he was eventually able to argue his case before the Supreme Court in the landmark *Brown v. Board of Education* trial. Marshall called on the Clarks to provide testimony based on their research and the results of the Doll Test. A recent

Attorneys George E. C. Hayes, Thurgood Marshall, and James Nabrit Jr. celebrate their victory in the Brown v. Board of Education *case on May 17, 1954.*

95   "Kenneth and Mamie Clark Doll," *National Park Service*, April 10, 2015, https://www.nps.gov/brvb/learn/historyculture/clarkdoll.htm.

96   https://www.youtube.com/watch?v=tkpUyB2xgTM.

biographical article on the Clarks noted the 1920s and 1930s had been psychology's "era of scientific racism," and that the Clarks had come along at "literally the height of a period in psychology marked by the study of racial differences in intelligence, presumed to be innate and biologically based," yet that their work "was quite influential as part of the integrationist case in the *Brown v. Board* decision. It was also the first time social science research was used in a Supreme Court Case."[97]

The Clarks' evidence was convincing. The court ruled that segregation of schools was unconstitutional. Chief Justice Earl Warren wrote that "in the field of public education the doctrine of 'separate but equal' has no place" because segregated schools were "inherently unequal"[98] and that legal separation of Black children resulted in "a feeling of inferiority as to their status in the community that may affect their hearts and minds in a way unlikely to ever be undone."[99]

In 1955, the Supreme Court met in a follow-up case: *Brown v. Board of Education II*. Although the court had mandated desegregation the previous year, no plan had been determined to carry out the ruling. Chief Justice Warren left much of the responsibility in the hands of local school authorities and lower courts that had originally heard school segregation cases, ordering them to implement the first *Brown* decision with full compliance and "with all deliberate speed."[100]

STUDENT PIONEERS

Just because segregation was now unconstitutional did not mean the integration of schools was going to be easily implemented. And even though the highest court in the land had said to act quickly did not

97   Alexandra Rutherford, "Developmental Psychologist, Starting from Strengths," cited in McNeill.

98   "Brown v. Board of Education," History.com, April 8, 2020, https://www.history.com/topics/black-history/brown-v-board-of-education-of-topeka.

99   "Kenneth and Mamie Clark Doll."

100   "Brown v. Board of Education of Topeka (2)," *Oyez*, https://www.oyez.org/cases/1940-1955/349us294.

mean that all local officials were going to comply. The law had changed, but not prevailing attitudes. The first Black students to attend previously all-white schools had to endure ridicule, threats, intimidation, and even acts of violence. Below are a couple of examples.

The Little Rock Nine shake hands with Robert F. Wagner Jr., mayor of New York City in 1958.

The Little Rock Nine

One of the first tests of the desegregation decision took place in 1957 in Little Rock, Arkansas. Nine African American students, pictured above, enrolled in what had been, until then, all-white Central High School. But three weeks had gone by, and they had not been able to set foot in the school yet. Each time they tried, they were met with an enraged mob of protesters, spouting racial slurs and shouting, "Two, four, six, eight, we ain't gonna integrate." Arkansas governor Orval Faubus dispatched the National Guard, but not to protect the young people. It was ordered to prevent the Black students from entering.

The military presence escalated as President Eisenhower trumped Faubus's forces by sending 1,200 soldiers from the Army's 101st Airborne Division to see the students safely into school each morning and out in the afternoon. In between, however, the nine vastly outnumbered Black students were on their own. The youngest of the nine, fourteen-year-old Carlotta Walls, recalls, "I learned early that while the soldiers were there to make sure the nine of us stayed alive, for anything short of that, I was pretty much on my own." She describes the nine of them being ridiculed with names like "baboon," having books knocked from their hands, and other acts of harassment and abuse.

When the nine students refused to back down, successfully integrating Central High, the next year Governor Faubus took even more extreme action and closed *all* of Little Rock's public high schools. Carlotta took her eleventh-grade classes by correspondence but returned the next year to become the first Black female graduate of Little Rock's Central High. Shortly before graduation, someone bombed her house. Refusing to be intimidated, she was at school the next day. She later published a memoir of her experiences titled *A Mighty Long Way*.[101]

Ruby Bridges

Breaking the longstanding racial barriers in schools was traumatic enough for nine Black teenagers who had one another for support. Imagine what integration was like for a six-year-old girl becoming the only Black child in a grammar school.

Ruby Bridges was attending a segregated kindergarten in New Orleans when the state was required to integrate. The grammar schools devised an entrance exam for African Americans to determine whether they were academically capable of keeping up with white students. The test was very difficult, clearly intended to justify continued segregation, but Ruby passed it. The scene outside her grammar school was much like that outside Central High for the Little Rock Nine: crowds of angry white parents screaming insults and holding racist signs. Every day, as seen below, federal marshals accompanied Ruby through the mob and into the school, two in front and two behind.

---

101   Lina Mai, "'I Had a Right to Be at Central': Remembering Little Rock's Integration Battle," *Time*, Sept. 22, 2017, https://time.com/4948704/little-rock-nine-anniversary/.

When the crowd intimidation did not crush Ruby's spirit, the white parents of children who would have been in Ruby's class withdrew their children. Ruby spent her first year in a class by herself with a faithful and dedicated teacher (a Boston native) who not only taught the daily lessons but also helped her learn to navigate the difficulties she was facing as a result of integration. During that year, her family suffered as well. Among other difficulties, her father lost his job, her grandparents were evicted from their sharecropping farm, and her mother was turned away from grocery stores.[102]

Six-year-old Ruby Bridges descends the steps of William Frantz Elementary School in New Orleans, Louisiana, accompanied by US Deputy Marshals in November 1960.

Despite having no one to eat with or play with the first year, Ruby never missed a day of school. By the next year, it seemed that the community had reluctantly accepted integration. Parents began to send their children back to class, the US Marshals were recalled, and

102 Debra Michals, "Ruby Bridges," *National Women's History Museum*, 2015, https://www. womenshistory.org/education-resources/biographies/ruby-bridges.

Ruby walked to school by herself. Eventually other students began to talk and play with her.[103]

Ruby Bridges and the Little Rock Nine were two of the first—and most prominent—examples of segregation. As thousands of Americans saw the rage of the communities where these young people were only trying to go to school in compliance with *Brown v. Board of Education*, a lot of the viewers' attitudes toward integration began to shift.

But keep in mind that similar scenes were taking place in thousands of communities across the nation. Many, many other young Black people had to endure indignities, oppression, insults, and violence for years to come. School integration would continue to be a divisive social issue for a long while, but thanks to these first student pioneers, a cultural shift had begun.

MARCHING—AND DYING—FOR CHANGE

The problem was that the Supreme Court had made a ruling for desegregation, but there was no clear plan to carry it out. Without any federal backing to enforce *Brown v. Board of Education*, the enforcement was left to the individual states, so the results were very diversified. Some states, especially those in the South, were resistant and slow to respond, and their schools remained segregated.

In response, groups organized a series of marches on Washington to draw attention to the need for integration. The tactic had worked in the early 1940s to protest unequal working opportunities for African Americans and to encourage desegregating the military.[104] When people hear "March on Washington," they typically think of the 1963 rally that we will examine later in this chapter. But that was not the first one. Prior to that, there were two Youth Marches for Integrated Schools.

---

103   "Ruby Bridges," *Biography*, June 22, 2020, https://www.biography.com/activist/ruby-bridges.

104   Jessie Kindig, "March on Washington Movement (1941-1947)," *BlackPast*, Dec. 6, 2007, https://www.blackpast.org/african-american-history/march-washington-movement-1941-1947/.

The first was in 1958 when ten thousand people, both Black and white, marched on Washington to promote equality and integration in schools. They were led by Coretta Scott King, Jackie Robinson, Harry Belafonte, and others. Belafonte took a group of students to the White House, asking to meet with President Eisenhower, but the request was denied. Dr. Martin Luther King Jr. had planned to attend, but he had recently been stabbed with a letter opener by a deranged lady at a Harlem book signing. He had been rushed to the hospital and was still recovering, so his wife spoke on that occasion and did an excellent job.

(A doctor later told Dr. King that the blade of the weapon had been so close to his aorta, that if he had sneezed, he would have died. Two ribs and part of his breast plate had to be removed during the four-hour surgery. He was twenty-nine at the time. A decade later, he spoke about what he would have missed seeing "if I had sneezed" as he gave his "I've Been to the Mountaintop" message the day before he was assassinated.)[105]

Another march was organized the next year, and Dr. King spoke to a crowd of twenty-six thousand people. Again, the march brought together Black and white students and adults who were promoting improvements. At the time, some people on both sides were resistant to integration. For African American students, it could be a logistics issue; many had to travel long distances to their new (previously all-white) schools, sometimes requiring their school days to be from daylight until dark.

Stronger resistance, however, came from the whites—not just in the South but in the North as well. Many, such as those pictured to the right, were simply opposed to "mixing the races." The word race, as it was being used during this time, essentially denoted a separate species. Once people had formed that misconception, it

105 DeNeen L. Brown, "Martin Luther King Jr. Was Stabbed by a Deranged Woman. At 29, He Almost Died," *The Washington Post*, Jan. 21, 2019, https://www.washingtonpost.com/history/2019/01/21/martin-luther-king-jr-was-stabbed-by-deranged-woman-he-almost-died/.

only made sense that whites should stay with whites and Blacks with Blacks. Little if any acknowledgment was made that we really are the same people. That is why there were laws in so many states at the time that forbade marriage between Blacks and whites. They were not supposed to come together.

That is also why initial steps toward integration were often met with such violent resistance, even after being mandated by the

Protesters in Little Rock, Arkansas, rally against integrating Central High School in 1959.

attacked. Many students had to be watched and supervised by law enforcement and military personnel. Much of the backlash that resulted was directed at members of the NAACP because it was the organization that had raised the money to hire the attorneys to argue the case for integrated schools. An extended and fierce retaliation was carried out from 1955 to 1966, resulting in many bodily assaults against and even murders of several NAACP members and associates:

» Z. Alexander Looby and Arthur Shores were both attorneys invested in the rights of African Americans and frequently associated with the NAACP. Both had their homes bombed, but both survived.

» Fannie Lou Hamer has been compared to Martin Luther King Jr. for her ability to inspire listeners. Angered by efforts to deny African Americans the right to vote and for other injustices, she got involved in organizing and registering young voters. One evening in 1962 after taking a group to register, only to be denied because of an unfair literacy test, their bus was stopped by police on the way home and fined $100. The bogus charge was that the bus was "too yellow." That night she was fired from her job as a plantation worker and had much of her property confiscated.

RETALIATION AGAINST NAACP:

» Z. Alexander Looby
» Arthur Shores
» Fannie Lou Hamer
» Rev. George Lee
» Medgar Evers
» Louis Allen
» Vernon Dahmer

The next year she and several other Black women were sitting in a "whites-only" restaurant at the bus station. They were arrested and taken to jail, where Fannie and several of the others were beaten severely—so much so that Fannie had permanent injuries to her eye, kidney, and leg. Yet she was not deterred from her convictions and created an organization that recruited hundreds of Black and white college students to help African Americans register to vote in the South.[106]

---

106 Debra Michals, ed., "Fannie Lou Hamer," *National Women's History Museum*, 2017, https://www.womenshistory.org/education-resources/biographies/fannie-lou-hamer.

» Rev. George Lee, Medgar Evers, Louis Allen, and Vernon Dahmer were all killed in separate incidents in Mississippi, largely because they were active in both exercising their right to vote and signing up other African Americans to do so. Most had some connection with the NAACP, which brought down the wrath of white supremacists. Many crimes, even murders, were committed at will with no consequence against the white assailant. Space does not allow going into detail about their lives and accomplishments, but I encourage readers to research these courageous people and many others who stood up for civil rights during this turbulent time, even at the risk of their own lives.

Still, positive progress was being made as a result of their struggles. One welcome achievement was the Twenty-fourth Amendment in 1964 that abolished the poll tax. Previously, a tax had been imposed that had to be paid before people were able to vote. Poll taxes made it more difficult for many Blacks and poor whites to vote. The Supreme Court ruled the poll tax to be illegal and struck it down in the Twenty-fourth Amendment.

Dr. Martin Luther King Jr. delivers his "I Have a Dream" speech to a crowd of approximately 250,000 in Washington, DC, in 1963.

MARTIN LUTHER KING'S DREAM

Many African American preachers were instrumental in providing motivation and encouragement for Black people as they sought to achieve social justice. They understood that spiritual justice and social justice were intrinsically linked. They did not want social justice to become their theology, but they were committed to applying their theology to their social environments.

One of the most prominent speakers throughout this period, as I have already mentioned, was Dr. Martin Luther King Jr. One of his most powerful orations was the "I Have a Dream" speech delivered in 1963 at a rally to challenge whites, Blacks, and Latinos in the United States to come together for freedom and jobs. An estimated 250,000 people gathered at the Lincoln Memorial to hear him speak—as seen in the photos above—and call the nation into accountability.

I want to make several observations about this speech, and the first couple I would like to address to fellow pastors and preachers. With all the speakers to be heard on August 28, 1963, the requested time limit was seven minutes. Dr. King prepared a speech in accord with the same limits as less notable speakers. When we give significant forethought to what we want to say and how we want to say it, we do not have to go on and on and on.

However, my second point is the importance of spontaneity. As it turned out, Dr. King had not intended to deliver the "I Have a Dream" speech in Washington. He had prepared something different to say. But one of his singers had heard him give a version of the Dream speech on a previous occasion in Detroit, and asked him to tell that great crowd of people about his dream. He must have thought it was a good idea because it is now remembered as one of history's most significant orations. He ended up speaking closer to sixteen minutes, but he held that crowd in rapt attention the entire time.

Let us look at some of the specific strengths about this speech. No fewer than eight times he declared, "I have a dream." Each time, it registered not only with his Black and Latino listeners, but with everyone who by this time had witnessed the consequences of racial prejudice and discrimination. Hundreds of thousands of people, many of whom were standing there that day, were dreaming of a more civil, compassionate, and equal relationship between white people and peoples of color.

You really need to find this speech and read it slowly, word for word. Better yet, listen to a recording of King delivering it himself.[107] The whole speech is powerful, and you will get a better appreciation for what Dr. King was calling for.

After a one-sentence "happy to be here" greeting, Dr. King noted the significance of the date:

> Fivescore years ago, a great American, in whose symbolic shadow we stand today, signed the Emancipation Proclamation. This momentous decree came as a great beacon light of hope to millions of Negro slaves who had been seared in the flames of withering injustice. It came as a joyous daybreak to end the long night of their captivity.[108]

---

107 "Top 100 Speeches," *American Rhetoric*, https://www.americanrhetoric.com/speeches/mlkihaveadream.htm.

108 This and subsequent quotations from the "I Have a Dream" speech are from *I Have a Dream: Writings and Speeches That Changed the World*, Martin Luther King, Jr., Edited by James M. Washington (New York: Harper Collins, 1986, 1992), pp. 102-106.

To begin with, King notes that it has been one hundred years since Lincoln signed the Emancipation Proclamation. In 1863, that declaration had been heard and received with a tremendous sense of relief and hope for a better future. But as we have already noted several times, the anticipated progress for people of color did not advance at the rate that should have occurred. Dr. King immediately stated that very point:

> But one hundred years later, the Negro still is not free; one hundred years later, the life of the Negro is still sadly crippled by the manacles of segregation and the chains of discrimination; one hundred years later, the Negro lives on a lonely island of poverty in the midst of a vast ocean of material prosperity; one hundred years later, the Negro is still languished in the corners of American society and finds himself in exile in his own land.

We need to understand that the perception of many people in 1963 was that slavery had been over for a hundred years. Those who had benefited from the post-war economic growth and increasing financial security had little if any understanding of fellow Americans who had endured the Black codes, the Jim Crow laws, lynchings, the ever-present threat of the Ku Klux Klan, and other realities of life for Black communities. They had no sense of the frustration felt by so many others who had been promised equality—by the authority of the United States Supreme Court no less—back in 1865 and 1877, but were still to see the fruition of those promises that had been either ignored or repealed. The remarks of Dr. Martin Luther King Jr. were resonating with a large and attentive audience. He continued:

> In a sense we've come to our nation's capital to cash a check. When the architects of our republic wrote the magnificent words of the Constitution and the Declaration of Independence, they were signing a promissory note to which every American was to fall heir. This note was the promise that all men, yes, black men as well as white men, would be guaranteed the unalienable rights of life, liberty, and the pursuit of happiness.

It is obvious today that America has defaulted on this promissory note in so far as her citizens of color are concerned. Instead of honoring this sacred obligation, America has given the Negro people a bad check; a check which has come back marked "insufficient funds." We refuse to believe that there are insufficient funds in the great vaults of opportunity of this nation. And so we've come to cash this check, a check that will give us upon demand the riches of freedom and the security of justice.

Dr. King spoke the unvarnished truth: It was as if Black people had been given a "bad check" by their government. Crucial promises had been broken. Yet he also chose to remain confident and hopeful. America was not bankrupt. There was more than enough justice and freedom to go around. Change was necessary, yet there were right and wrong ways to effect that needed change:

> There will be neither rest nor tranquility in America until the Negro is granted his citizenship rights. The whirlwinds of revolt will continue to shake the foundations of our nation until the bright day of justice emerges.

> But there is something that I must say to my people who stand on the warm threshold which leads into the palace of justice. In the process of gaining our rightful place we must not be guilty of wrongful deeds.

> Let us not seek to satisfy our thirst for freedom by drinking from the cup of bitterness and hatred. We must forever conduct our struggle on the high plane of dignity and discipline. We must not allow our creative protest to degenerate into physical violence. Again and again we must rise to the majestic heights of meeting physical force with soul force.

When people of color eventually are rightfully acknowledged, Dr. King urged them not to then begin to oppress others, not to be guilty of "wrongful deeds." Despite the accumulated disappointment and frustration of the past centuries, violence was not an appropriate response. "Creative protest" was an acceptable strategy; physical violence was not. Yet now that many had begun to become more vocal in their quest for integration and equality, King knew that lots of their critics were beginning to ask, "When will you be satisfied?" He provided the answer:

> We can never be satisfied as long as the Negro is the victim of the unspeakable horrors of police brutality. We can never be satisfied as long as our bodies, heavy with fatigue of travel, cannot gain lodging in the motels of the highways and the hotels of the cities. We cannot be satisfied as long as the Negro's basic mobility is from a smaller ghetto to a larger one.

> We can never be satisfied as long as our children are stripped of their selfhood and robbed of their dignity by signs stating "for whites only." We cannot be satisfied as long as a Negro in Mississippi cannot vote and a Negro in New York believes he has nothing for which to vote. No, we are not satisfied, and we will not be satisfied until justice rolls down like waters and righteousness like a mighty stream.

That last phrase is straight out of the Bible. The prophet Amos had a lot to say about justice—or more specifically, the lack of it he was seeing in the culture of his time, even among God's people. The difference was that the Israelites had abandoned justice; they were apathetic about it. Those in the civil rights movement, however, were passionate about seeing justice done because they had been denied it for so long. They echoed Amos's desire: "Let justice roll on like a river, righteousness like a never-failing stream!" (Amos 5:24, NIV)

Dr. King further answered the "When will you be satisfied?" question when he arrived at the "I have a dream" portion of his speech. This portion was packed with specifics:

> Even though we must face the difficulties of today and tomorrow, I still have a dream. It is a dream deeply rooted in the American dream. I have a dream that one day this nation will rise up and live out the true meaning of its creed—we hold these truths to be self-evident, that all men are created equal.

I have a dream that one day on the red hills of Georgia, sons of former slaves and sons of former slave owners will be able to sit down together at the table of brotherhood.

I have a dream that one day, even the state of Mississippi, a state sweltering with the heat of injustice, sweltering with the heat of oppression, will be transformed into an oasis of freedom and justice.

I have a dream my four little children will one day live in a nation where they will not be judged by the color of their skin but by the content of their character. I have a dream today!

I have a dream that one day, down in Alabama, with its vicious racists, with its governor having his lips dripping with the words of interposition and nullification, that one day, right there in Alabama, little black boys and black girls will be able to join hands with little white boys and white girls as sisters and brothers. I have a dream today!

I have a dream that one day every valley shall be exalted, every hill and mountain shall be made low, the rough places shall be made plain, and the crooked paces shall be made straight and the glory of the Lord will be revealed and all flesh shall see it together.

Again, Dr. King returns to the imagery of Old Testament prophecy to illustrate his point. The prophet Isaiah wrote of a voice calling, "In the wilderness prepare the way for the Lord; make straight in the desert a highway for our God. Every valley shall be raised up, every mountain and hill made low; the rough ground shall become level, the rugged places a plain. And the glory of the Lord will be revealed, and all people will see it together. For the mouth of the Lord has spoken" (Isaiah 40:3-5, NIV). The comfort that God was offering His people then (Isaiah 40:1) was what Dr. King was directing to the various states of the racist South of the 1960s. This was a very, very godly statement about a social agenda to push forward.

As I previously suggested, please look up this speech and read it for yourself when you have time to give it some serious thought. It has inspired many people throughout the decades, and continues to do so. Coretta Scott King, the wife of Dr. Martin Luther King Jr., once commented on this speech: "At that moment it seemed as if the Kingdom of God appeared. But it only lasted for a moment."[109]

The August 28, 1963, March on Washington for Jobs and Freedom was indeed a memorable moment in American history, but few people know exactly how special it was. Prior to the march, both Dr. King and President Kennedy had expressed grave concern for what kinds of trouble might break out that day. Since the previous May, there had been 1,340 demonstrations in more than two hundred cities in response to scenes out of Birmingham where police dogs had been loosed on Black protesters and fire hoses turned full-force on Black children. Now, with hundreds of thousands of frustrated and agitated people assembling in Washington, many were expecting the worst.

Kennedy provided more security than for any other peacetime event in US history. The FBI was called in to support the Secret Service, including 150 agents mixed in among the crowd. The Washington police force was on highest alert, and created a response plan for seventy-two envisioned disaster scenarios. The National Guard was called in to support police in providing protective details for Congress, national monuments, and stores that might be looted. Local judges were placed on call for expected trials, and jails were evacuated to make room for problematic protesters. Hospitals canceled plans for elective surgeries to free up 350 beds for emergencies. Government offices were closed and employees told to stay home. The city imposed a twenty-four-hour ban on alcohol—the first since Prohibition. The five military bases nearby were put on high alert with fifteen thousand special forces ready to deploy and thirty helicopters to fly them in if needed. President Kennedy had executive orders prepared ahead of time, one to order the crowd to disperse and another authorizing the Pentagon to take "all appropriate steps"

---

109 Ibid., p. 102.

to break them up if necessary. One report noted: "The city was transformed from the capital of a nation at peace to a nation at war."

Many other precautionary preparations were made as well, but they were all unnecessary as Dr. King spoke powerfully about his dream and the importance of nonviolent change to improve the lives of African Americans. At the end of the day, only three arrests had been made—all involving whites. The police chief's most important order of the day was for his officers not to eat the prepared box lunches because the chicken had been sitting out all day.

That day in 1963 no banks were robbed. Nobody was rushed to the hospital. It was a riot that never happened.[110]

Why are we still off-base about race? I suspect too many people today are living by the old standard of "an eye for an eye and a tooth for a tooth." Dr. King taught and modeled what could be accomplished by an unwavering commitment to nonviolent commitment to change, and at the time, hundreds of thousands of people listened to him. Can you conceive of a gathering today of 250,000 frustrated protesters standing in the heat all day without a single incident of violence?

---

110 Nick Bryant, "Martin Luther King and the Race Riot That Never Was," BBC News, Aug. 25, 2013, https://www.bbc.com/news/magazine-23790147.

9

White Sacrifice...
Unsung Heroes

Sometimes we talk about how Black history has been written out of history books, but I believe we also overlook many instances where whites have helped Blacks without proper acknowledgment. We need to increase our awareness of such instances.

One such white person was Walter Reuther, president of the United Automobile Workers (UAW) from 1946 until 1970. Pictured at the right, he not only worked to provide better benefits and working conditions for laborers, but also he was an active advocate for civil rights. He supported equal rights for Blacks and whites within the Union, moved to advance Blacks, funded and

Walter Reuther, president of United Automobile Workers from 1946 until his death in 1970, put righteousness and equality into practice.

supported the advancement of Blacks in our society, and helped them with legal issues. He participated in the March to Selma, and the UAW financed the 1963 freedom marches in Detroit and Washington.

Reuther was one of the few non-African American speakers at the Washington rally. When he began to speak from the platform, one of the marchers leaned over and asked a friend, "Who is Walter Reuther?" He was told, "Walter Reuther? He's the white Martin Luther King."[111] Reuther was somebody who believed in righteousness and equality, as well as putting them into practice.

BLOODY SUNDAY

This was a volatile era for African Americans who actively worked for their civil rights, as well as for the whites who supported and aided them in their efforts. During the 1960s, much effort was being made to persuade Blacks to register and vote. Their rights were being denied through poll taxes, required intelligence tests, and other illegal or unscrupulous means.

During a night march in Marion, Alabama, to protest the arrest of a fellow activist, twenty-six-year-old Jimmie Lee Jackson was marching with his sister, mother, and eighty-two-year-old grandfather. When the nonviolent protesters began to be attacked by the local police force supported by state troopers, they ran for shelter in various homes, businesses, and the church they had just come from. Jimmie and his family went into a nearby café but were followed by police who began to beat his mother. As a good son, former soldier, and the youngest deacon in his church, Jimmie tried to protect her. An Alabama state trooper responded by shooting him in his stomach, and then chased him into the street and beat him until he collapsed. Jimmie died eight days later, but during that time Dr. Martin Luther

---

111   Thomas Featherstone, "No Greater Calling: The Life of Walter P. Reuther," *Wayne State University Library*, http://reuther100.wayne.edu/bio.php?pg=4.

King Jr. went to see him, and Jimmie was able to hear the civil rights hero praise his courage and faith.

No case was brought against the Alabama trooper—at least not for a long while. He was eventually indicted for the shooting, but it was over forty years later. Jackson's death was later called "the catalyst that produced the march to Montgomery" on what would come to be known as Bloody Sunday, just over two weeks later.[112]

The fifty-four-mile march—a scene from which is pictured below—

An unidentified Canadian clergyman joins Dr. Martin Luther King Jr. and his family on the march from Selma to Montgomery in 1965.

was planned from Selma to Montgomery, protesting injustice in a county where African Americans comprised more than half the population, but only two percent of the registered voters. The leaders intended to take their case directly to Governor George Wallace in the state capital. Wallace told state troopers to "use whatever measures are necessary to prevent a march," yet six hundred started out on Sunday, March 7. They proceeded through downtown Selma without

---

112 "Jackson, Jimmie Lee: Biography," *Stanford University Martin Luther King, Jr. Research and Education Institute*, https://kinginstitute.stanford.edu/encyclopedia/jackson-jimmie-lee.

problem and started over the Edmund Pettus bridge (named for a Confederate general and purported grand dragon of Alabama's Ku Klux Klan). As the first marchers crested the bridge, however, they saw state troopers and local police assembled and waiting on the other side.

When they got closer, an announcement over a bullhorn warned them to disperse. Marchers were expecting violence, so they got in an

John Lewis and Hosea Williams lead marchers across the Edmund Pettus Bridge in Montgomery, Alabama, on "Bloody Sunday," March 7, 1965.

almost single-file line crossing the bridge, following march leaders John Lewis and Hosea Williams—both of whom are pictured above. The police and troopers began to attack them with clubs, whips, and rubber tubing wrapped in barbed wire. Lewis was struck in the head; the blow caused a cracked cranium, but fortunately he was not killed. He lived to become a congressman and lifelong advocate of Black rights. The attackers were also wearing gas masks and using tear gas on the marchers. Onlookers stood back and cheered as they watched. What was so noteworthy about this protest was that the marchers had committed not to fight back. When they could no longer move forward due to the violent and malicious treatment they received, they had no choice but to fall back the way they had come.

However, this event was one of the first such civil rights abuses filmed by television crews on the scene. By the time the footage had been flown to New York and processed, it was late that evening, but networks still interrupted their scheduled programming to show it. As it so happened, the feature on ABC that night was *Judgment at Nuremberg*, a program about the horrendous treatment and imprisonment of the Jews during the Holocaust. Nearly fifty million viewers witnessed the government-sanctioned beatings and bleeding of non-violent protesters amid the smoke of tear gas in Alabama, suddenly juxtaposed with the atrocities of Nazi history. The visual impact of the scene resulted in sit-ins, traffic blockades, demonstrations, and other signs of solidarity across the country.[113]

The evening after the Bloody Sunday attack on the marchers, Dr. King sent out a flurry of telegrams and public statements "calling on religious leaders from all over the nation to join us on Tuesday in our peaceful, nonviolent march for freedom." President Lyndon Johnson soon added his endorsement: "Americans everywhere join in deploring the brutality with which a number of Negro citizens of Alabama were treated when they sought to dramatize their deep and sincere interest in attaining the precious right to vote."[114]

The march was scheduled again for March 21, this time with the accompaniment of federalized National Guard troops. By the time the marchers completed their four-day march and arrived in Montgomery, the crowd of supporters had grown to twenty-five thousand. Public opinion had shifted. Less than five months later, Congress had passed the Voting Rights Act. When President Johnson signed

113   Christopher Klein, "How Selma's 'Bloody Sunday' Became a Turning Point in the Civil Rights Movement," History.com, July 18, 2020, https://www.history.com/news/selma-bloody-sunday-attack-civil-rights-movement.

114   "Selma to Montgomery March," *Stanford University Martin Luther King, Jr. Research and Education Institute,* https://kinginstitute.stanford.edu/encyclopedia/selma-montgomery-march.

it into law, he called the day "a triumph for freedom as huge as any victory that has ever been won on any battlefield."[115] Within months of its passage, a quarter of a million new Black voters had been registered. Within four years, voter registration in the South had more than doubled.[116]

After Dr. King's call for action, both Blacks and whites began to respond. I want to pay special attention to the response of white America. Thanks to the media, many were just beginning to view what African Americans had been forced to live with for many decades. Too often when we revisit history and see the many conflicts between Blacks and whites, we oversimplify them by declaring one group right and the other group wrong. But in this case, many white Americans responded to King's call—not because they themselves were affected by what was going on, but because those injustices were affecting our entire nation and their understanding of who God is.

INDIVIDUALS TO REMEMBER

I do not believe white America has been properly acknowledged for their contributions to the civil rights movement as they came alongside Black Americans and joined their struggle because they thought it was godly and righteous. I do not want that era of history to be remembered as merely a Black vs. white conflict.

We all need to see that when one of us is being treated unjustly, we are all being treated unjustly. We are called by God to practice righteousness not only for ourselves but also on behalf of other people who are being treated unrighteously. Believers need to become a united front to resist ungodly behavior.

---

115 "Voting Rights Act of 1965," *Stanford University Martin Luther King, Jr. Research and Education Institute*, https://kinginstitute.stanford.edu/encyclopedia/voting-rights-act-1965.

116 Eunice Hyon Min Rho, "Remembering Dr. King's Defense of Voting Rights," ACLU.org, Jan. 16, 2012, https://www.aclu.org/blog/voting-rights/promoting-access-ballot/remembering-dr-kings-defense-voting-rights.

Below are a few white Americans who paid the highest price in their defense of African Americans during this turbulent and chaotic era of Black struggle.

James Reeb

Reverend James Reeb was a white pastor from Boston, Massachusetts, who responded to the call of Dr. Martin Luther King Jr. for religious leaders to support the nonviolent protest for voting rights. He was a thirty-eight-year-old husband with four kids. He graduated from Princeton with a degree in Sacred Theology—one of the highest degrees one could get at the time—and ministered in both the Presbyterian and Unitarian Church. He chose to reside in a low-income neighborhood and enroll his children in public schools where many of the students were Black. He was also a youth director at the YMCA to help people who did not have all the privileges he had.

He wasted no time going South after witnessing the events of Bloody Sunday on March 7, 1965, and was having dinner with two other ministers in an integrated restaurant in Selma on March 9. Coming out of the restaurant that evening, several men crossed the street and began to beat them severely with baseball bats. All three were injured, but Reeb received a traumatic head injury that led to bleeding from his brain. He was transferred to a Black hospital that was not as well equipped as most of the white hospitals. Despite the severity of his injury, a nearby white hospital refused him admittance because he had been standing up for African Americans, and he lost two hours as he was taken for help to Birmingham. He slipped into a coma and died two days later.

Three white men were indicted for Reeb's murder, but acquitted. In Reeb's eulogy, Dr. King said that Reeb "symbolizes the forces of good will in our nation. He demonstrated the conscience of the nation. He was an attorney for the defense of the innocent in the court of world opinion. He was a witness to the truth that men of different races and classes might live, eat, and work together as brothers."[117]

Viola Liuzzo

Mrs. Viola Liuzzo, pictured to the right, was a thirty-nine-year-old wife with five kids from Detroit, Michigan, although she had grown up in the South. As a member of the Detroit chapter of the NAACP, she was aware of the Southern conflicts and injustices, and she had witnessed the violence of the Bloody Sunday march on a news broadcast. Two weeks later, she was in Selma, Alabama, despite the fact that in that interval she had heard what segregationists had done to James Reeb.

Viola Liuzzo was shot twice in the head by members of the KKK while she shuttled protesters back and forth between Selma and Montgomery.

Liuzzo was using her own car to shuttle protesters back and forth between Selma and Montgomery to advocate for voting rights for African Americans. She was carrying an African American teenager and fellow worker named Leroy Moton along Route 80 when she stopped for a red light. A car pulled up beside her, Ku Klux Klan members pulled out weapons, and they shot her twice in the head, killing her. Her car ended up in a ditch. Moton was covered in her blood, so he played dead but would later testify against the shooters, three of whom were sentenced to ten years in prison.[118] They served

---

117 "Reeb, James," *Stanford University Martin Luther King, Jr. Research and Education Institute,* https://kinginstitute.stanford.edu/encyclopedia/reeb-james.

118 "Viola Gregg Liuzzo Biography," *Biography,* Nov. 19, 2020, https://www.biography.com/activist/viola-gregg-liuzzo.

time for a federal charge of conspiring to intimidate African Americans, but no one was ever officially charged with her murder.

The facts of this event came to light because one of the men in the KKK car was an FBI informant. But more than that, he was a KKK member whom the FBI was paying for information . . . and he was suspected of taking part in the murder. This cold-blooded slaying of a white mother of five was certain to attract a great deal of attention, and within hours, FBI Director J. Edgar Hoover had quickly contrived a cover story. The cuts on her arm from the car window's shattered glass were said to indicate "recent drug use." In addition, the report asserted that she was a bad wife and mother who had abandoned her family to go South, and that she was having an affair with nineteen-year-old Moton.

Liuzzo's family knew better, of course, and contested the findings. But it was not until 1978 after using the Freedom of Information Act that her family could officially clear her name. Her autopsy showed no traces of drugs in her system or recent sexual activity. And in her journal that was released by the FBI, she had written, "I can't sit back and watch my people suffer." An interviewer had to ask why a white woman would write that about Black people, and the now-grown daughter clarified, "She actually believed it when Christ said that the suffering and needy are our people. Mom saw all other human beings as her people."[119]

(This smear campaign was a black mark on the FBI because the leader at the time was desperate to hide the fact that they had been financing one of Liuzzo's killers. However, after having served as a chaplain for the FBI and seeing first-hand the incredibly challenging situations faced by their agents and the victims they work with, I am certain it is currently a credible and honorable organization.)

---

119   Donna Britt, "A White Mother Went to Alabama to Fight for Civil Rights. The Klan Killed Her For It," *Washington Post*, Dec. 15, 2017, https://www.washingtonpost.com/news/retropolis/wp/2017/12/15/a-white-mother-went-to-alabama-to-fight-for-civil-rights-the-klan-killed-her-for-it/.

Viola Liuzzo was the only white female killed in the civil rights movement. Many historians believe her murder was instrumental in the rapid passage of the Voting Rights Act passed on August 6, 1965. Five decades after her death, she was honored with an award from the Birmingham Civil Rights Institute on its twenty-fifth anniversary. She is included among forty martyrs on the Civil Rights Memorial in Montgomery. She was also inducted into the Michigan Hall of Fame in 2006.

Both James Reeb and Viola Liuzzo became active after the Bloody Sunday incident. They were aware of the violence and the intimidation by both the police and white supremacists. Yet they willingly got involved and paid the ultimate sacrifice in seeking a solution to the unrighteousness of racism.

Jonathan Daniels

Jonathan Daniels, pictured to the right, was in his second year of seminary at Episcopal Divinity School in Cambridge, Massachusetts, when he heard the call of Dr. Martin Luther King Jr. for the clergy to get involved in civil rights. Now twenty-six, he had been the valedictorian at Virginia Military Institute. He and a fellow seminarian arrived in Alabama on a Thursday, planning to be back in classes Monday morning, but they stayed for

Seminary student Jonathan Daniels was killed by a bullet meant for one of his companions—a Black female demonstrator—in August 1965.

nearly a week and then determined to return and stay longer. Daniels wrote, "Something happened to me in Selma, which meant I had to come back. I could not stand by in benevolent dispassion any longer without compromising everything I know and love and value. The imperative was too clear, the stakes too high, my own identity was called too nakedly into question. . . . I had been blinded by what I saw here (and elsewhere), and the road to Damascus led, for me, back here."

Daniels and his fellow student decided to live and work in Alabama during that semester. He wrote about his daily life: "Sometimes we take to the streets, sometimes we yawn through interminable meetings . . . . Sometimes we confront the posse, sometimes we hold a child." The two returned at the end of the semester to take final exams, and Daniels visited his family in New Hampshire. He went back to Alabama while his friend went to fulfill a school requirement in Missouri.

In Alabama, Daniels lived with a Black family in Lowndes County, where he was welcomed as one of them. The county had a reputation for violence-enforced segregation. One morning he was part of a group of thirty people—mostly local young African Americans— protesting discriminatory hiring practices and unequal treatment of customers in Hayneville. The police were prepared to arrest them, and at the same time, they were approached by a group of white men carrying guns, clubs, and broken bottles. Before things got out of hand, they were all arrested and taken to jail on a flatbed truck usually used for hauling garbage.

The protesters were confined in the jail for six hot August days without air conditioning, showers, or toilets. Daniels led hymns and prayers, and did what he could to encourage the group. While there, he happened to share a cell with noted civil rights leader Stokely Carmichael, who had been arrested on a different charge. After six days, Carmichael made bail and left for Selma. A short time later, the jail guards unlocked the doors and told them to leave, giving no explanation. No bail had been posted.

They were ordered to leave jail property while waiting for a ride, so Daniels accompanied Catholic priest Richard Morrisroe and two Black demonstrators, Joyce Bailey and Ruby Sales, to a nearby store to buy soda for the group. They did not anticipate trouble because mixed groups had been to that store before. However, they were met by Thomas Coleman, a construction worker and part-time deputy, carrying a shotgun. Coleman ordered them to leave but did not wait for them to respond as he leveled his gun at seventeen-year-old Ruby Sales. Daniels pushed her out of the way and received the blast intended for her, dying instantly. Morrisroe was wounded, yet Coleman shot him again, in the back. He required hours of surgery, but he lived. These two men decided to risk their lives to protect two young women because it was the right thing to do as Christians. Coleman was acquitted by a jury and died in 1997 at the age of eighty-six. But the twenty-six-year-old man he shot died on the street that day.[120]

These three examples of white sacrifice all came from the same era of history and have been acknowledged for their selfless and courageous commitment to the rights of others. But throughout history, a other white people have been bold enough to oppose Black oppression. You may remember Omaha's mayor, Ed Smith, from Chapter 7, who was almost lynched when he tried to prevent the unjust killing of a Black prisoner in his city. That was 1919, but there have certainly been many other unacknowledged white supporters of Black rights who saw past the prejudices and unjust treatment of their peers and took brave stands for righteousness, regardless of the cost.

I want to operate like the people I have described. I want to carry myself with the respect, compassion, and courage they demonstrated. I want to lay my head down at night and know I have done the right

120 Mary Frances Schjonberg, "Remembering Jonathan Daniels 50 Years after His Martyrdom," Episcopal News Service, Aug. 13, 2015, https://www.episcopalnewsservice.org/2015/08/13/remembering-jonathan-daniels-50-years-after-his-martyrdom/, and "Jonathan Daniels, Civil Rights Hero," *Virginia Military Institute*, https://www.vmi.edu/archives/genealogy-biography-alumni/featured-historical-biographies/jonathan-daniels-civil-rights-hero/.

things. Amid all the controversy, the anger, and all the other sin in our society right now, God calls us to do the right things at the right times. Even when scared and threatened, we can do what is right and stand against injustice without rioting. God has blessed most of us to a point where we could live very comfortable lives removed from the injustices others regularly face, but instead, let us choose to do something for someone else. You do not need to be a member of the clergy or a mayor to do the right thing; you can be a student or a housewife. And doing the right thing will not always require pain and loss. Sometimes people (like Walter Reuther) find much security and satisfaction when they are willing to spend their lifetimes devoting their time, talents, and resources to make this world a better place. The main requirement is willingness.

Why are we still off-base about race? Taking an unpopular stand on behalf of disenfranchised peoples can involve risk—not usually the risk of life as seen in this chapter, but more commonly a risk to personal reputation or social status. It is easier and safer to observe— or even to write a check for the cause—than to get actively involved in the ongoing struggle for justice and equality for all. As we turn our attention to theology, let us ask God to send workers to this ripe field of opportunity.

10

God's Perspective on Race

Throughout this book so far, I have tried to demonstrate that what most people usually define as "race" is a terrible misperception. No one would deny the clearly observable differences in people's physical features (nose size, lip size, fine vs. coarse hair, and above all, skin color). It is bad enough that somehow society has determined that some of those features are more desirable than others as standards of beauty. Even worse, however, we have seen that throughout history certain physical traits have been used to determine that one group of people is more intelligent, or more capable, or more entitled than another.

We saw in the early chapters that these observable differences (phenotypes, if you recall the term), are deceptive. In reality, all human beings, regardless of skin color, hair color, eye color, or whatever, are 99.9 percent alike. The concept of "race" is a mirage, and we need to stop seeing significant differences that do not really exist.

In Chapter 2, I challenged you to ensure that your theology influences your sociology (how you interpret your observations and pre-judgments), and not allow your sociology to influence your theology. In this chapter, I want to examine in more depth how theology should affect how we deal with issues of "race." Some of these observations have already come up, but here I want to provide a more cohesive look at Scripture to emphasize the equality and worth of all people in the eyes of a righteous and loving God.

GOD'S PLAN FROM THE BEGINNING

The Genesis account shows that humanity was created by God from only two people. We all belong to the same parents. The whole issue of race is founded only on small variations over time in our DNA that have nothing to do with our humanity. Everyone who professes belief in the Lord is part of God's family—we are children of God. No one is more important or less important than anyone else in this family. "There is neither Jew nor Greek, there is neither slave nor free, there is no male and female, for you are all one in Christ Jesus" (Galatians 3:28).

After Creation, and particularly after a "restart" of humanity after the great Flood, God's instructions to Noah were: "Be fruitful and multiply and fill the earth" (Genesis 9:1). Yet we saw in Chapter 3, that all humans continued to exist in the same space, speaking the same language. Then, in blatant defiance, they started constructing the Tower of Babel to "make a name for ourselves, lest we be dispersed over the face of the whole earth" (Genesis 11:4). It was the point where humanity decided to become as powerful as God, to be like God, to be as important as God is.

I am convinced one of the major sins people commit today is trying to get rid of the God who holds them accountable: a God of conviction, a God who tells them they are wrong, a God who defines the problem as sin. It is hard for the church to speak clearly about sin when so many people justify their personal beliefs and behaviors. But the reality is that God is still sovereign over the earth and has declared certain actions to be sinful. We have no authority to take God's place and change what He has declared sinful or not sinful.

In response to the people's defiance at the tower, God confounded the language of humanity. What He had brought together, He decided to separate (for a while). He understood that if He changed language, He would change culture, ethnicity, and how people bonded together. If they no longer spoke the same language, it would create separation which soon became segregation. God implemented separation by causing language change which resulted in the emergence of different ethnicities.

Bonding within smaller groups led to breeding within smaller groups. The size of the gene pool was significantly reduced. Therefore, cultural likenesses also became biological likenesses over time. People groups begin to look alike. We have interpreted those differences in appearance as race, but they are not. They are only the logical result of a restricted gene pool. As we are beginning to see, when those segmented groups begin to intermarry, you no longer have such dramatic separation by biology, or in culture.

The point is that the Lord initiated ethnicity because of the wickedness in the hearts of humanity, but He did not intend it to go on forever. He had already planned the arrival of His Son Jesus on earth as the only solution that could forgive and repair our wicked hearts. After providing a remedy for the sin and wickedness of people, God was then able to begin to reunite those He had previously separated. When we were separated by our sin, Jesus came to bring us back together again.

We also saw in Chapter 3 that in Jerusalem on the Day of Pentecost, God assembled people of all languages and ethnicities and the Holy Spirit enabled them to hear the same message at the same time (Acts 2:7-12). God separated us for our own good, and then God brought us back together. I believe the coming of the Holy Spirit on the Day of Pentecost was to enable us to eradicate the erroneous beliefs and opinions that have separated us from one another. We should continue to depend on the power of the Holy Spirit as we commit to tearing down everything that separates and divides us: racism, injustice, ethnicity issues, oppression, discrimination, and prejudice.

One of Jesus' last instructions to His followers was to respond to the Holy Spirit: "You will receive power when the Holy Spirit has come upon you, and you will be my witnesses in Jerusalem and in all Judea and Samaria, and to the end of the earth" (Acts 1:8). It is okay to celebrate our ethnicities, but not to take inappropriate pride in one over another. God does not want us cherishing our distinctions to the point of ignoring our unity in Christ Jesus. Every person on every continent in every culture is my brother or sister in Christ. I must not let cultural or ethnic pride prevent me from sharing the love of God with everyone.

The apostle Paul puts this incredible work of God into clearer perspective:

> Therefore remember that at one time you Gentiles in the flesh, called "the uncircumcision" by what is called the circumcision, which is made in the flesh by hands—remember that you were at that time separated from Christ, alienated from the commonwealth of Israel and strangers to the covenants of promise, having no hope and without God in the world. But now in Christ Jesus you who once were far off have been brought near by the blood of Christ. For he himself is our peace, who has made us both one and has broken down in his flesh the dividing wall of hostility by abolishing the law of commandments expressed in ordinances, that he might create in himself one new man in place of the two, so making peace, and might reconcile us both to God in one body through the cross, thereby killing the hostility (Ephesians 2:11-16).

We were Gentiles, uncircumcised, separated, alienated, strangers, with no hope, without God—what a list! No matter how far away from God we get, Jesus can reconcile us with God—and then with our human brothers and sisters. Christ can resolve the pain that has arisen from oppression and racism and bring us back together in relationship. I am still excited about being Black, and I want everyone to be excited about their own ethnicity, whatever it is. But the thing we all should be most excited about is that we are now a "new creation" in Christ Jesus (2 Corinthians 5:17), and together we become a new ethnicity in Him. We now belong to the ethnicity of God, which brings us into relationship with people whom we might have previously considered outsiders or adversaries just because they look different.

HARD LESSONS

This was the lesson Jonah had to learn the hard way. Most of us know the part of his story about being swallowed by the great fish, but many times we miss the main point. God told him to go to Nineveh to call the people there to repentance, but Jonah set sail for Tarshish in the opposite direction. Why this bold act of disobedience?

Nineveh was the capital city of Assyria, and Assyria was an unspeakably cruel and merciless enemy. In reviewing an art exhibit depicting some of their historic warfare, the writer says:

> Assyrian art contains some of the most appalling images ever created. In one scene, tongues are being ripped from the mouths of prisoners. That will mute their screams when, in the next stage of their torture, they are flayed alive. In another relief a surrendering general is about to be beheaded and in a third, prisoners have to grind their fathers' bones before being executed in the streets of Nineveh.[121]

Israel was soon going to be among the conquered, and Jonah had no desire to heed God's instructions to: "Arise, go to Nineveh, that great city, and call out against it, for their evil has come up before me" (Jonah 1:2). Many people assume that Jonah did not want to go to Nineveh because he was afraid of what might happen if they did not listen to him. But that was not the case. After God used a terrible storm and a great fish to turn Jonah around and do as instructed, the whole city of Nineveh repented. Their response irritated Jonah to no end, as seen in his frustrated prayer:

> O Lord, is not this what I said when I was yet in my country? That is why I made haste to flee to Tarshish; for I knew that you are a gracious God and merciful, slow to anger and abounding in steadfast love, and relenting from disaster. Therefore now, O Lord, please take my life from me, for it is better for me to die than to live (Jonah 4:2-3).

Jonah was not afraid the people of Nineveh would not listen to him; he was afraid they would! When they began to repent, he refused to show a whit of compassion for them, and he did not want God to, either. While in the belly of the fish, he had been most appreciative

---

121 Jonathan Jones, "'Some of the Most Appalling Images Ever Created'—I Am Ashurbanipal Review," *The Guardian*, Nov. 5, 2018, https://www.theguardian.com/artanddesign/2018/nov/06/i-am-ashurbanipal-review-british-museum.

and thankful that God had shown mercy on him, but he was greatly dismayed when God's mercy extended to Israel's enemies.

He found a spot outside Nineveh and made himself comfortable, hoping to see God's wrath pour down on the city. God provided a leafy plant to sprout up and furnish shade for him, which made Jonah "exceedingly glad." But then God provided a worm to eat through the plant and kill it. The sun beat down and Jonah grew faint. Again, he told God, "It is better for me to die than to live" (Jonah 4:5-8). As Jonah pouted in the heat of the sun, God pointed out the obvious: Jonah was more concerned about his personal comfort than for the lives of more than 120,000 people and all their animals.

The animosity and hostility between the Assyrians and Jews was not exactly like the racial issues we continue to face today, but the lesson is the same. When wronged by someone, do we pray for "justice" when we really mean revenge? When an adversary gets COVID, do we rejoice, or do we pray for God to heal the person?

If we get more focused on what is good for "me" than what's best for "us," we are never going to arrive at a point of mutual respect and equality. Whatever racial issues we are facing, our theology should pull us back to God's righteousness, grace, and mercy.

As difficult as it can be, we need to learn to ask for God's forgiveness rather than revenge. Certainly, we should take bold stands for justice and oppose oppression wherever we see it, but we must resist letting our emotions get out of control. Scripture is filled with exhortations to be more forgiving by remembering how much God has forgiven us. Here is one such reminder from Paul:

> Do not grieve the Holy Spirit of God, by whom you were sealed for the day of redemption. Let all bitterness and wrath and anger and clamor and slander be put away from you, along with all malice. Be kind to one another, tenderhearted, forgiving one another, as God in Christ forgave you (Ephesians 4:30-32).

I know this is not a popular message. In response to all the injustice and oppression that many of us have faced, it is understandable that we want to justify our anger and resentment, but the gospel just does not teach that. The gospel calls us—in all our ethnicities—to come together as one, under our Lord and Savior Jesus Christ.

CORPORATE IDENTITY

Americans have traditionally taken pride in being rugged individualists, but that mindset can be harmful, particularly when dealing with racial problems. Rather than dwelling too long on questions like "What's in this for me?" or "What did I do wrong?" or "Who did I offend?" we need to be more concerned about "What have we done wrong?" Our theology reminds us that God's people have a corporate identity. It was true for the people of Israel, and for the church today.

What does corporate identity entail? It means I am connected to everyone around me, including their failures and sins. We do not mind praying for God's corporate blessing on our church, city, nation, or world. But when it comes to confessing wrongdoings, we tend to be quick to bail out and point fingers at people we feel are worse than we are.

As God was preparing to lead His people out of the wilderness and into the Promised Land, their first major obstacle would be the walled city of Jericho. Before engaging in conflict, Joshua warned the people, "Keep yourselves from the things devoted to destruction, lest when you have devoted them, you take any of the devoted things and make the camp of Israel a thing for destruction and bring trouble upon it. But all silver and gold, and every vessel of bronze and iron, are holy to the Lord; they shall go into the treasury of the Lord" (Joshua 6:18-19).

But after the walls of the city fell and the Israelites rushed in to claim victory, a man named Achan took two hundred silver coins, a bar of gold, and a nice robe, and buried them in his tent. No one noticed—no one, that is, except God. The next battle against Ai should have been an easy win, especially after the magnificent victory at Jericho. But no. The Israelites were easily repelled, and as they were retreating, thirty-six of them were killed. Joshua was distraught and asked God what had happened. God told him someone had stolen some of the things that were to be set apart for God. Lots were drawn to determine the guilty party, and Achan confessed.

Like God had warned, Achan's sin had affected the whole camp. Thirty-six men were dead as a result, camp morale had bottomed out, and their rejoicing over Jericho had turned to mourning. The consequences were harsh. Achan and his entire family (who were complicit in his theft) were stoned to death (Joshua 7). It demonstrated just how important attention to corporate identity could be. When I was growing up, people used to say, "Keep your family name pure. Don't disgrace your family." They understood corporate identity and connection.

A more positive example is that of Isaiah. When God was calling him to be a prophet, he was shown the glories of God's lofty throne surrounded by heavenly attendants. The moment was too much for Isaiah, surrounded by smoke, flying angels, and high-volume worship that shook the building. He said, "Woe is me! For I am lost; for I am a man of unclean lips, and I dwell in the midst of a people of unclean lips; for my eyes have seen the King, the Lord of hosts!"

But one of the angels flew to the altar, picked up a burning coal with a pair of tongs, and touched the coal to Isaiah's lips, saying, "Behold, this has touched your lips; your guilt is taken away, and your sin atoned for." God then asked, "Whom should I send, and who will go for us?" Newly cleansed, Isaiah immediately responded, "Here I am! Send me" (Isaiah 6:1-8).

Isaiah identified with his people. He did not try to present himself as better than the rest of them. As a prophet, he could continue to associate himself with the increasingly sinful Israelites. I too want to be a mouthpiece for my people, the church, with corporate identity.

I want to make every effort to connect to everybody else in God's family. That starts by repenting of my sins and the sins of my people, stepping forward, and asking for God's mercy. I need God to purify my mouth, so that my guilt will be taken away and sin atoned for.

As we have seen, God has called us to go to the uttermost parts of the world and proclaim the truth of the gospel. We cannot do that if we are harboring feelings of racism and prejudice. We need to ask God to deliver us from racism. If you have been a victim who has been hurt, I pray for your healing. If you have been acting in wickedness and ungodliness, I pray for God to remove permanently the hatred and violence from your heart. I pray that everyone who reads these words will be saturated with the love of God, respond with repentance, and experience God's healing in their lives.

While we are considering Isaiah's heavenly vision, let's look at a portion of John's vision as recorded in the book of Revelation:

> After this I looked, and behold, a great multitude that no one could number, from every nation, from all tribes and peoples and languages, standing before the throne and before the Lamb, clothed in white robes, with palm branches in their hands, and crying out with a loud voice, "Salvation belongs to our God who sits on the throne, and to the Lamb!" (Revelation 7:9-10).

Ultimately, this is God's view of race. This is what heaven will look like. People of all nations, tribes, and languages are in front of the throne of God. Everyone has the same cleansing and white robes. The blood of the Lamb has brought them together as one people. Whether we ever resolve our racial differences here on earth or not, we are surely going to be together up there.

TWO GOALS

When challenged to prioritize the importance of God's laws, Jesus had a ready answer: "You shall love the Lord your God with all your heart and with all your soul and with all your mind. This is the great and first commandment. And a second is like it: You shall love your neighbor as yourself. On these two commandments depend all the Law and the Prophets" (Matthew 22:37-40).

If we seek to love God with heart, soul, and mind, we can neither participate in nor overlook racism. We cannot even pretend to love God if we do not show love for our fellow humans (1 John 4:20-21). And learning to love our neighbors as ourselves gives us two goals: (1) To get along better with our believing brothers and sisters, and (2) To introduce as many nonbelievers as possible—including "strangers and aliens"—to the love, forgiveness, and mercy of Jesus Christ. This is what the Lord has called us to do. This is our mandate.

Every time we say the Lord's Prayer, we pray for God's will to be done on earth as it is in heaven. Our job as believers is to bring heaven to earth. This is the theology that should drive everything else. It is the way to healing of past wounds, changing of improper attitudes, and new commitments to forgiveness and reconciliation. Otherwise, we are left to our best human efforts, and we've seen how that has worked out so far.

Why are we still off-base about race? Frankly, for many people, civil rights and racial matters are social issues rather than spiritual ones. I think we need to approach this vital topic with God's perspective. No matter how passionate we might be for the cause, we can be assured that God is even more desirous of seeing a wider demonstration of righteousness, justice, and equality among the people He has created, loved, and redeemed.

11

Specific Choices,
Courageous Steps
(Solutions)

I grew up in Chicago and went to college in downstate Illinois, which means I spent lots of hours on the interstate. Several times, the police pulled me over with no apparent provocation, or as they say today, for "driving while black." Each time was a harrowing experience.

One time the officer asked for my identification, and I quickly gave it to him. He went back to his car, checked me out, returned, and said, "Please step out of the car."

I asked, "What's the problem, sir?"

He got visibly angry and growled, "Step out of the car right now!"

As I got out, I told him, "I'd like to know what this is about."

Instead of answering me, he said, "Turn around and put your hands on the roof of the vehicle."

Again, I asked, "Officer, I just want to know what's happening here."

He walked back to his patrol car, leaned in, and came back wearing a pair of leather gloves—not the kind to keep your hands warm . . . the kind you put on for a street fight. I said, "Sir, I'm not looking for any trouble. I just want an explanation."

He walked back to the car again, radioed to dispatch that he was having problems with someone he had pulled over, and asked for backup. Within minutes, five cars rolled in with their lights flashing. The officers surrounded me. It looked as if they were ready to take me down! Then, an older officer, maybe forty-five years old, approached me with no malice on his face and asked, "How are you doing?"

I responded, "Sir, I'm kind of upset. I'm not sure what's going on here. I can't get an answer to a simple question about why I was pulled over."

He replied, almost quietly, "It appears that your driver's license is suspended."

I was very surprised. I told him, "I'm not sure how that could happen. As far as I know, it's still good."

He asked, "What address is on your license?"

"My home in Chicago," I replied.

He explained, "Well, it looks like you got a ticket for an expired license plate, which I'm guessing was sent to your home address. It's probably sitting on your dresser at your parents' house. Your parents probably didn't tell you, or they didn't open your mail, so you missed your court date. When you missed the date, your license was suspended, and the court issued a warrant for your arrest." He paused to let this news sink in, and then he said, "Come with me and get in my vehicle. We'll go to the station and get all this worked out."

As we crossed the street to his car, he put his arm around me. I glanced back and saw that the officer who first pulled me over was fuming with rage! He jumped up and down, screaming at me: "You should be arrested for resisting arrest! This isn't right!"

I could not take my eyes off the belligerent police officer, but within seconds, I was in the other officer's patrol car. When we got to the station, he contacted the court to set a new date for me, and he released me under my own recognizance.

Of course, all the officers surrounding me that day were white. The first one was eager to show me who was boss. If he had followed procedure and told me why he was stopping me, perhaps we could have resolved the problem very easily. The other officer, though, stepped into a threatening scene, spoke calmly to deescalate the situation, and treated me with respect. I can imagine that he took a lot of heat from the first officer, who undoubtedly criticized him and tried to tarnish his reputation. At significant cost to himself, the second officer refused to racially profile, refused to treat a Black man with suspicion, and chose to extend common courtesy to someone who looked different.

Years later when I applied to be a chaplain for the FBI, I was concerned about the litany of stops listed on my record, but the agent interviewing me just shook his head and said, "All of these infractions were without probable cause. Both of us know what that's about. It's no problem for us."

I related this story because as we begin to consider solutions for the vast racial divide in our country today, I want to begin by saying there is often only so much one person can do. In my encounter with that first officer, I do not believe I could have done anything more to avoid arrest. The officer saw a Black man with a warrant out on him, and that is all the information he cared about. But when another officer was willing to listen to the other side of the story, the truth emerged, and the tense situation was resolved.

You can only do so much, that is true, yet any hope of improving racial relations begins with more of us doing what little we can do. Healing has to start somewhere. Why not with you? Below are some suggestions for getting started.

A WELCOMING ATMOSPHERE

Racial divisions can affect you as part of a church, a member of a secular group, or as an individual. After racial gaps have formed, and perhaps have existed for a long time already, how do we begin to close them? How do we begin to portray a more godlike spirit and a more godike nature?

A welcoming atmosphere starts with hospitality. We sometimes think of hospitality as a nice little ceremony like having neighbors over for coffee and cake. That is not inaccurate, but it is a bit simplistic. Hospitality is a biblical concept that includes personal effort, including friendliness, generosity, and a willingness to serve. Hospitality goes beyond our families and personal friendships and reaches out to the stranger who may be in need. It motivates us to cross divides and express the love of God with intentionality, doing for others what God has done for us. God loved us first, and we return that love to Him by loving others, appealing to others in friendship, understanding their importance, and being a giving person.

We need to stop thinking about people in our communities or those who occasionally drop into our churches as mere visitors; we should treat them as guests. Good hotels do not cater to visitors; they prepare for guests. Hospitality includes anticipating others' needs and letting them know how important they are through good service and friendly conversation. Christians and Christian ministries must become a welcoming culture, a culture that reaches out with intentionality to ensure that all people, whatever their ethnicity or culture, feel affirmed.

Then, building on hospitality, we continue to cultivate a welcoming spirit with friendship. You have probably known people who are very hospitable, yet never really show a desire for any deeper level of involvement. Friendship requires authenticity and vulnerability. In racial issues, especially, we will need to go deeper than just a few surface conversations.

As hospitality is extended and friendships are formed, we can go one step further and increase our generosity, having a spirit of giving and caring for other people. For example, envision a church which ensures that greeters do not just stand at the door and shake hands, but one which has people out in the parking lot waving banners and welcoming guests as they arrive. Imagine them sending representatives out into the community regularly to let everyone know that this church affirms them and desires their presence, making a special point to welcome people who are poor, disadvantaged, and homeless because God is a welcoming God.

At Jesus' crucifixion, His arms were stretched wide as He hung on the cross, and those outstretched arms remind us of His willingness to take in the world. He died so the world might have life, and have it more abundantly. We too should be more willing to cultivate a culture of welcoming to all peoples, both as individuals and collectively as the church. We can initiate conversations and ask questions to better understand what makes people feel welcome and what makes them feel drawn to our lives and ministries.

What makes people feel drawn to you? Some people have a naturally welcoming spirit and work hard to develop an authentic welcoming culture. Others carry themselves a certain way or have body language that prevents others from getting very close. Some people think, *That's just who I am. I'm just a serious person.* The truth is, that is a learned behavior. People often do not realize how often they are frowning or looking upset, or what opportunities they are missing because others are reluctant to approach them.

We must be purposeful about developing a welcoming culture, which includes the willingness to hear constructive criticism. If people are reluctant to offer suggestions or let you know you unintentionally did something wrong, that is an indication that you push people away and you do not have a welcoming spirit. If you are not sure, it is easy enough to find out. Start by asking a few people you know well, "Do I have a welcoming culture? Do you feel a sense of welcoming when you come into my presence?" Then you can ask the bigger question: "How do you think I relate to strangers, or people who are different from me? Do I make them feel welcome and make them feel God's presence?"

Before we can make strides toward resolving our racial tensions, old and long-standing walls may need to be torn down. One of the strongest divisions throughout Scripture was that between the Jews and the Gentiles. Centuries of history and tradition had pushed them further and further apart. Yet Jesus' sacrificial death made possible their reconciliation:

> For he himself is our peace, who has made us both one and has broken down in his flesh the dividing wall of hostility by abolishing the law of commandments expressed in ordinances, that he might create in himself one new man in place of the two, so making peace, and might reconcile us both to God in one body through the cross, thereby killing the hostility (Ephesians 2:14-16).

The King James Version refers to the "wall of hostility" as "the middle wall of partition." In our dealings with other ethnicities, some people feel a lot less hostility than others, but most of us would have to admit the walls are still standing between us that need to be demolished. One sure way to tear down the middle wall of partition between yourself and others is to start by being friendly and generous, and then to develop a consistent welcoming spirit.

A CULTURAL STRATEGY

After creating a welcoming atmosphere, we can work on developing a cultural strategy. This begins with an awareness of cultural IQ or CQ. You are probably familiar with IQ (intelligence quotient), a number that is determined by taking a specially designed test. Likewise, CQ is a similar assessment, but one based on culture rather than intelligence. It is a measure of our ability to create cultural competency with other people. The value of understanding and respecting other cultures is important for a number of reasons. Here is one example of how it can affect business interactions:

You see them at international airports like Heathrow. Posters advertise the global bank HSBC, showing a grasshopper and the message:

USA—Pest.

China—Pet.

Northern Thailand—Appetizer.

Culture is so powerful it can affect how even a lowly insect is perceived. So it should come as no surprise that the human actions, gestures, and speech patterns a person encounters in a foreign business setting are subject to an even wider range of interpretations, including ones that can make misunderstandings likely and cooperation impossible. But occasionally an outsider has a seemingly natural ability to interpret someone's unfamiliar and ambiguous gestures in just the way that person's compatriots and colleagues would, even to mirror them. We call that cultural intelligence or CQ.

Cultural intelligence is related to emotional intelligence, but it picks up where emotional intelligence leaves off. A person with high emotional intelligence grasps what makes us human and at the same time what makes each of us different from one another. A person with high cultural intelligence can somehow tease out of a person's or group's behavior those features that would be true of all people and all groups, those peculiar to this person or this group, and those that are neither universal nor idiosyncratic. The vast realm that lies between those two poles is culture.[122]

If businesses realize the benefits of understanding and respecting other cultures and ethnicities, how much more should we be willing to do so to reduce the levels of racial tension in our society. We need

---

122 P. Christopher Earley and Elaine Mosakowski, "Cultural Intelligence," *Harvard Business Review*, October, 2004, https://hbr.org/2004/10/cultural-intelligence.

to build bridges that allow us to move into other cultural groups and converse with them, engage them, and acknowledge their value. You can value someone as a person without necessarily endorsing his or her attitudes, behaviors, and religious beliefs. That ability to interface with people of different cultures is your CQ.

How, exactly, do you do that? Most of us have more opportunities to improve our CQs than we realize. Every time you attend a workshop or find yourself in a classroom setting, look for opportunities to start conversations with people from other cultures. Commit to regular involvement in a civic group, book club, volunteer organization, or church ministry which puts you in contact with people outside your usual circle of friends. Be more diverse in your choices of movies and television programs. Several recent Oscar winners have provided enlightening insights into other cultures. Once you begin to see how beneficial it is to understand and appreciate other peoples' backgrounds, you will become more and more aware of other opportunities that can expose you to cultural realities outside your own personal experience.

The more you start to reach out to people who are different from you, the more you will begin to grow spiritually. You are not challenged until you see how different some people are and how much your love needs to grow. It is much easier to love someone who already knows and understands you—and who usually loves you back. We think we are doing fine. But when we start to encounter new people and unfamiliar situations, we see how much we still need to grow.

Increasing your CQ can also help improve your conflict management skills—it takes you beyond mere conflict resolution. Some issues will not get resolved, so you need to know how to manage conflict. It is difficult to handle a conflict that you do not understand in the first place. Managing conflict requires more skill when you are dealing with people who think differently than you do, act differently than you do, and express their emotions differently than you do.

Conflict management is a crucial aspect of developing a cultural strategy. I have found it very helpful in church settings. The church must create a formal means of teaching people to interact with and learn from one another, which also requires a strategy for how conflict will be addressed and resolved—particularly conflict between people with different cultural backgrounds.

Conflict will arise from time to time, so churches need to have steps in place for how to respond when it does. It may be difficult for some people, but conflict management will often involve confrontation with someone. Being confrontational does not mean becoming angry, imposing your will on someone else, or looking for a fight. It does mean, however, we should not ignore injustices just because speaking up might make us feel awkward or insecure. If we identify racism, oppression, or other relational sins, we need to do everything in our power to restore holiness and righteousness.

I was recently in a meeting when someone began to make derogatory comments about an entire nation of people. It was not my nation, or where my people were from, but his statements were untrue and unjust. I responded: "I think it's inappropriate to color a whole nation of people and suggest they all act only one particular way. That would be like saying it's in their DNA, and that would mean God created them that way." The topic changed and the meeting went on. I do not know if I changed the person's opinions at all, but I felt I needed to say something to refute what he was saying.

EMBRACE A GODLY VISION

As we create a welcoming atmosphere and develop a cultural strategy, we begin to model what it means to embrace a godly vision. Especially when people are in conflict, godliness may be the last thing on their minds. They might get upset when someone speaks a language they do not understand, or looks or dresses much differently from what is considered "normal," or practices a custom that is not necessarily wrong, but just different. Their confusion and frustration in the moment takes their focus away from God's will and God's glory. Those are the situations when we need to remember that we are all created in the image of God—to embrace a godly vision about how we see and understand others.

Paul said it like this:

> For though I am free from all, I have made myself a servant to all, that I might win more of them. To the Jews I became as a Jew, in order to win Jews. To those under the law I became as one under the law (though not being myself under the law) that I might win those under the law. To those outside the law I became as one outside the law (not being outside the law of God but under the law of Christ) that I might win those outside the law. To the weak I became weak, that I might win the weak. I have become all things to all people, that by all means I might save some. I do it all for the sake of the gospel, that I may share with them in its blessings (1 Corinthians 9:19-23).

That is what you call embracing a godly vision! Sometimes we want to present the gospel, but we do not take the time to understand the person who needs the gospel. The better we know someone, the more effective our presentation of the gospel will be.

Embracing a godly vision includes acknowledging every person's connection to God. *Imago Dei* is Greek for "image of God"—it is a phrase that applies to every human being. As different as humans may appear, we all have the same red blood, the same internal organs, the same genetic makeup. Why? Because God created the first pair of humans in His image (Genesis 1:27), and every human today still bears that image. We need to celebrate that connection we have with God—and with one another.

A second aspect of embracing a godly vision is enforcing justice for all. Whenever we see unjust things happening to other people, we step in to help them and do our best to ensure the injustice comes to an end. The church is in a great position to respond to injustice—to organize people and march on city hall, to make presentations in groups, and to hold in context what is right. Individuals should do the same, but the church can turn out in greater numbers. We cannot let injustice just keep happening.

Justice is to be shared. It is not enough to demand it for myself; I must also want others to receive justice. Many people speak loudly and often about fairness and equality, but life does not dish out either one. It is often up to us to make sure fairness is shown to those who are oppressed or under attack from other people because we have a clearer awareness of the image of God in those people.

Sometimes we are too busy or self-absorbed to befriend someone of another ethnicity. Instead, we settle for shallow, token relationships. We stay within our own ethnic comfort zones and never venture out to see how other cultures live, work, and relate. We fear conflict and retreat into silence. Worst of all, we are so shortsighted that we never see our fellow human beings as God does: as equally loved and valued. We need to create a welcoming atmosphere, develop a cultural strategy, and embrace a godly vision. When we do, we will see much-needed changes begin to take place.

Why are we still off-base about race? Often it is because we want to do something but just do not know where to begin. I hope the suggestions in this chapter will give you a good start to making positive changes in your relationships with those of other ethnicities.

12

Final Exam (Ask Yourself)

If you have made it to this point in this book, I applaud your discipline and persistence. I realize many people would have preferred to jump right into proposed solutions and quick-and-easy answers to the racial struggles that continue to divide us. Instead, I wanted you to see how those problems came to occur in the first place. If you see how ingrained they have become in our society, you will not come to expect quick-and-easy answers. Finding lasting solutions is neither quick nor easy.

By now you have read through several "classes" of background information: biology, sociology, theology, and others. (History class was particularly long and packed with significant events, yet space limitations required that we leave out much more than we were able to include. I hope you will continue to read and research your cultural past, whatever it is, on your own.)

The reason I took this approach is because I believe it is the best way to get to the root of the racial problems we are experiencing. Amid all the disagreements, struggles, and varying opinions about how to proceed, I hope I have provided enough to help you make informed decisions about how to proceed from here. You may not have all the answers you seek, yet you should have a much deeper understanding of the problem.

192 STILL OFF-BASE ABOUT RACE

We have seen that "race" is not a separation of species. Race is not the identification of biological differences that put us into different classes of humanity. The reality is that "race" is based on some very, very small differences in the way people look that have nothing to do with who we are, how we think, or how we behave. There is no biology connected to that, so we need to understand race in its place. Race is something we can use to identify ourselves, but it should not be used by others to identify us. In other words, you might identify yourself along certain racial lines, but I should never try to tell you who you are, using terms of race. Many of us may need to do some mending and some healing about how we have come to understand race. God created all of us in His image, and the biological differences between us are negligible. Regardless of skin color and other minor physical variations, we are all brothers and sisters.

So in this chapter, I encourage you to do a frank and honest self-examination. I have heard people say that minorities cannot be racist, but that's a fallacy. Anyone can be a racist, and we need to be honest about that fact. I doubt that any readers are going to admit to being full-fledged racists, yet I suspect that few will be able to deny ever having any racist leanings. The purpose of this exam is to see where you are on the spectrum of racism. The first section will ask you to look at your past, the second section addresses the present, and the third lets you anticipate future plans to reduce, if not eliminate, racism in your life.

Take your time and think through each question. Be specific and give as many specific examples as you can. (Additional questions can be found on the Personal Self-Assessment exercise on the Anti-Defamation League website. I have adapted material from them and added some of my own observations.)[123]

---

123 "Personal Self-Assessment of Anti-Bias Behavior," *Anti-Defamation League*, 2007, https://www.adl.org/sites/default/files/documents/assets/pdf/education-outreach/Personal-Self-Assessment-of-Anti-Bias-Behavior.pdf.

FINAL EXAM PART 1: YOUR PAST

1) To what extent have I tried to become educated about race?

   Have you sought out information about other cultures and peoples? Is it reliable information, or hearsay from others?

2) Have I examined my upbringing for biases?

   Have you objectively assessed the things your parents and other relatives taught you? Is the way you think and behave influenced by past untruths or half-truths about other ethnicities?

   I was once part of a team interviewing a young lady for an accounting job. She seemed highly qualified, yet at the end of the interview, the person I was interviewing with told me, "I have a problem with her."

   I asked, "What do you mean? Did she say something wrong? Did I miss something that was important?"

   I was stunned when she replied, "I don't believe I can work with a dot head" (referring to people from Eastern India). Even as qualified as that young lady was, and even with the diversity she would bring to the table, this person decided to discriminate. I do not believe her comment came out of thin air. I do not think it was even formed in her adulthood. I suspect her parents instilled in her a sense about people from Eastern India that created biases and racism of which she was not even aware. I confronted my teammate to her face about her racism and recommended the Indian woman get the job (and she did).

3) Have I combated others' racist behaviors? Or have I contributed to them?

   It takes some people longer than others to acknowledge racist behavior and begin to stand against it. We need to become bridges to righteousness and holiness, not just bypasses that ignore the problem. If we see racism and respond by ignoring it, smiling, or laughing, we contribute to the problem.

It is not enough to just be non-racist; we should be anti-racist. When we hear people say defamatory things about others, we need to challenge ourselves to respond appropriately. Any attack on a fellow brother or sister is really an attack on God, the Creator. When we denigrate the art, we are really criticizing the Artist.

4) Have I evaluated my language for hurtful words?

Do you tend to say things like, "All white people are this way," or "All Black people are that way"? What you may consider to be casual conversation may be heard by others as racist language.

Before I took a trip to Germany, I was a bit concerned about the way I might be treated as an African American there, based on their history. My preconceived racist fears influenced my thoughts and language about Germany and German people. As it turned out, however, I was treated better in Germany than any of the other European countries I visited. When I got there, they helped me with their language and went out of their way to accommodate me. They were outstanding hosts to this Black American citizen, so my preconceived notions and insensitive language were not only incorrect, but simply wrong. I learned a great deal from the experience because I allowed myself to be educated and change some of my erroneous presumptions.

5) Have I avoided stereotyping based on group identity?

Have you ever judged an entire ethnicity based on the actions of only a few people? Have you ever had a conflict with one person, and then taken your anger/frustration out on everyone who looked like him or her? If so, suppose you are stopped at a traffic light and are rear-ended by a guy driving a red car. Do you then make the presumption that everyone who drives red cars is a careless driver? Of course not. Yet sometimes we allow one bad experience with someone from another nationality or culture to influence our attitudes toward that whole country or people group. It makes no sense, yet it happens all the time.

FINAL EXAM PART 2: YOUR PRESENT

Now that you have taken a historical look at the possibility of racist tendencies in your life to this point, consider these questions about your current attitudes and actions.

1) Do I value others' cultures?

   Before you make any snap decisions about what other cultures eat or do, do you first study and understand the culture to find value where you can? Of course, sometimes you may run into beliefs or practices that are in direct contradiction with your own spiritual beliefs and understanding of Scripture, and you cannot agree on everything. Yet too often, people find other practices that do not conflict with what they believe, and then choose to denounce the "strange" culture anyway. Let us do the best we can to value other people's experiences and practices, and respect who they are.

2) Am I comfortable discussing racism?

   Talking about racial issues can be sensitive, emotional, and uncomfortable, but it should not be ignored. Talk to others about race. Find out how they feel. If they become upset, you do not have to participate in their anger, but your compassionate interest will usually open some doors to strengthen relationships.

3) Am I open to feedback about my behavior?

   Do people feel like they can approach you if they feel you have said something insensitive, or perhaps could have done a better job expressing your opinion about a controversial issue? Some of us have no intention to be racist, yet we use certain terms or comments that others find offensive. Sometimes, after a move to a different part of the country, the same language that was acceptable before is now met with resistance. Are you open to hearing that you might be hurting others with your words or behavior . . . perhaps without even knowing it?

   I once was appointed to a position, and the response I received from someone who was not African American was, "I affirm you for being a positive example of Affirmative Action." I, of course, did not feel the comment was appropriate. I felt that the very thinly disguised message was that I had received the position only because I was a person of color, and not as a result of my qualifications. I responded by asking if he knew anyone who was better qualified for the position. When he could not respond to that, I told him I felt his comment had been insensitive. He immediately apologized and said that he had not intended for me to take it that way. (I am not sure how else he thought I might have interpreted it, but at least I had evoked an apology and a reconciliation.)

4) Am I a voice for the oppressed?

When you see others mistreated, do you become proactive and engaged in seeing the problem resolved and justice done? Or do you remain silent? When you were a kid it may have been too frightening to stand up to a playground bully who was picking on someone else. But you are an adult now. If you are not responding to the oppression of others, find a way to address it and bring God's justice to an unjust situation.

5) Am I a biblical advocate?

You will also find yourself in situations that have nothing to do with oppression—for example, situations where God's voice needs to be heard and His will needs to be made clear. Do you speak up in those circumstances? The Bible says: "We who are strong have an obligation to bear with the failings of the weak, and not to please ourselves. Let each of us please his neighbor for his good, to build him up" (Romans 15:1-2). How well are you currently doing that?

FINAL EXAM PART 3: YOUR FUTURE

At this point, you cannot do anything about your past . . . except learn from it. An honest assessment of your current thoughts and behaviors can show you whether you are growing more sensitive to racial issues, sliding back into old habits, or remaining stagnant. Now, how you plan for the future can help ensure you continue to acknowledge and combat racial tensions that arise. Below are some commitments to consider as you look ahead to becoming a faithful advocate prepared to enact God's justice for everyone.

1) Will you have an unselfish vision of justice?

   Justice is often portrayed as a female holding scales that represent balance and fairness of issues. She is blindfolded so she cannot favor one side over the other. In issues of race, we should be blindfolded to our own biases and only able to enforce God's perspective. Is your desire for justice focused only on what is best for you . . . or for everyone involved?

   Racial inequality is often due to economic factors. How do you respond when you see people who are damaged? Those with privilege and position in society can provide help and hope for those who are often overlooked by offering financial support, mentoring, and other types of personal assistance. Without help, many poor people get lost in the system. Does your vision for the future include greater concern for the cheated, the poor, the fatherless, widows, and others in need? When people are being victimized, God is concerned. We should be, too.

2) Will you initiate biblical inclusiveness?

   Combating racism can become politicized, and does not necessarily align with scriptural teachings. Yet God calls believers to attend to the needs of "the least of these." He challenges us to seek out the forgotten and those who cannot repay our investments in them. God uses willing people to reach out to the overlooked, cast down, depressed, and unhappy. We can demonstrate the love of God by giving gifts, anonymously, to people who need them. That is what I mean by being biblically inclusive.

3) Will you represent your faith with appropriate symbols?

We often use symbols to reflect who we are and what we believe. What do you think when you see a star of David and a menorah? A crescent moon and star? A yin-yang circle? We see them on jewelry, wall plaques, bumper stickers, tattoos, and everywhere. In fact, the trendiness of such symbols can often lead to contradictory messages. If you cut someone off in traffic and he sees your Christian bumper sticker, what is he to think? When people visit, can they tell yours is a Christian home? As you interact with other cultures in the future, will you be aware of these nonverbal messages you are sending?

4) Will you look for the benefits of diversity?

It helps to overcome racism if we learn to see the advantages of our differences. There is a wealth of benefit in acknowledging and considering other cultural viewpoints—greater productivity as we learn new and different ways to do things, creativity as we see completely new perspectives that challenge us to try something different, and much more. But we are never likely to acquire such knowledge if we do not seek it out.

5) Will you see others as God sees them?

God sees qualities and gifts in people that no one else does. If we see God's image in them, they look different to us. God does not just see us today; He sees us tomorrow. God does not just see our failures; He sees our redemption. He does not just see our destruction; He sees our rebuilding. He sees what we are going to become, not just what we have made of ourselves in the past.

As you look at others who do not look like you, will you ask for God's vision, trying to see His divinity in them? Will you keep looking until you see their potential?

C. S. Lewis wrote:

> It is a serious thing to live in a society of possible gods and god-desses, to remember that the dullest and most uninteresting person you can talk to may one day be a creature which, if you saw it now, you would be strongly tempted to worship, or else a horror and a corruption such as you now meet, if at all, only in a nightmare. All day long we are, in some degree, helping each other to one or other of these destinations. . . . There are no ordinary people. You have never talked to a mere mortal. . . . It is immortals whom we joke with, work with, marry, snub, and exploit—immortal horrors or everlasting splendours.[124]

ONE FINAL LESSON

I would like to close this look at race with a true story. It is not a particularly happy ending for this book, but I believe it is a relevant one.

One day a young man (I will call him Randy.) rang the doorbell at our parsonage in Chicago. As soon as I opened the door, I could tell he was in trouble. He told me that he lived in a bad part of the city, and he had been involved in gangs, which meant he was deep into drugs and violence. He said that he wanted to straighten out his life.

As we spent time together, Randy committed his life to Christ and we prayed him through. I wanted to find him a role in our church, and to my surprise, he told me that he played the organ. Our people may have been suspicious of him at first, but they soon fell in love with him. In our supportive, loving environment, he grew in his faith. He was deeply grateful for the chance to start a new life with the people in our church, and he was very loyal to us.

From time to time, when executives from our denomination's International Office came to our church to speak and teach, Randy sat at the organ and played in their services. He was not a trained musician. He played by ear, so all he had to do was hear a song one time, and he could play it.

---

124 C. S. Lewis, *The Weight of Glory* (New York: HarperCollins, 1949), pp. 45-46.

At the time, I owned a security company in Chicago, and Randy expressed interest in launching a new career in this field. Though he had been involved in gangs, he had never been arrested, so his record was clean. He went through our training and served as one of our security officers. He enjoyed it, and soon his dream shifted to becoming a police officer.

Before he could go through the Police Academy, he was working one night when some rowdy men walked in. They caused a huge disruption, so Randy and a couple of his partners tried to stop them and usher them out the door. One of the men came back in, pulled out a weapon, and began randomly shooting people. Randy came in to try to stop him. When the gunman ran out the door, Randy ran after him, holstering his weapon because he was trained to value human life. He caught up with the man, tackled him, and took his gun away. He subdued the man and was holding him down until the police could arrive.

A police cruiser eventually pulled up outside, and a white officer got out. By this time, everything was under control, yet the arriving officer drew his gun as he entered the building. He jumped on top of the bar, yelled menacingly, and started pointing his gun at everybody there. Everyone was understandably terrified. Someone told him the shooter had run outside. He went outside and saw Randy holding the now screaming assailant. Other officers were beginning to arrive. The white officer pointed his gun at Randy and began yelling at him. People nearby screamed that he was a security officer who had stopped the attack, but without warning, the white officer fired repeatedly into Randy's back. Moments later, he died.

This event was shattering to me. Randy had done what all of us desperately wish and hope a wayward child or friend would do—he repented, found Christ, and found meaning and hope in a community of believers. He had planned to dedicate his life to prevent senseless crime, but before he could do that, he became a victim of it. That day, he had heroically protected innocent people, and he had peacefully subdued the assailant instead of shooting him. His death was so senseless, so unnecessary, so tragic.

I officiated at Randy's funeral. It was one of the saddest days of my life. I believe he died only because the white officer had an ingrained bias that shaped his perception of the situation. He assumed that the Black man on the scene must have been the perpetrator of the reported crime, not the courageous, skilled peacekeeper. And he used fatal force before waiting to ask questions and determine the truth.

I wish these biases and false assumptions were on the decline, but I fear they are not. We all see new, yet all too familiar, headlines far too often. So although I have tried to provide many explanations about why we are still off-base about race, and offer some optimistic strategies to improve Black/white relationships, I do not want to paint an overly rosy picture. We still have much work to do. We still need to get involved and make improvement where we can. Yet as we do, I can almost guarantee that you will be mistreated at some point.

Therefore, as we strive to serve God, let us remember that someday we will all share full equality in His kingdom. In the meantime, let us try to let go of as much resentment and frustration as possible as we work to establish a world of greater righteousness and peace.

Bibliography

"A Horrible Lynching," net: Nebraska's PBS & NPR Stations, Accessed Nov. 17, 2020. http://www.nebraskastudies.org/en/1900-1924/racial-tensions/a-horrible-lynching/.

"African American Senators." *United States Senate.* https://www.senate.gov/pagelayout/history/h_multi_sections_and_teasers/Photo_Exhibit_African_American_Senators.htm

"Andrew Johnson." *Britannica.* https://www.britannica.com/biography/Andrew-Johnson.

Barber, Kenneth E. "Johann Blumenbach and the Classification of Human Races," Encyclopedia.com

Bernard, Ian. "The Zong Massacre (1781)." *BlackPast* (Oct. 11, 2011). https://www.blackpast.org/global-african-history/zong-massacre-1781/.

Bhopal, Raj. "The Beautiful Skull and Blumenbach's Errors: The Birth of the Scientific concept of Race." *BMJ* (Dec. 22, 2007). https://www.ncbi.nlm.nih.gov/pmc/articles/PMC2151154/.

"Black Leaders During Reconstruction." History.com (Dec. 10, 2020). https://www.history.com/topics/american-civil-war/black-leaders-during-reconstruction.

Britt, Donna. "A White Mother Went to Alabama to Fight for Civil Rights. The Klan Killed Her for It." *Washington Post* (Dec. 15, 2017).

Brody, Richard. "The Worst Thing About 'Birth of a Nation' Is How Good It Is." *The New Yorker* (Feb. 1, 2013). https://www.newyorker.com/culture/richard-brody/the-worst-thing-about-birth-of-a-nation-is-how-good-it-is.

Brooks, Khristopher J. "Redlining's Legacy: Maps Are Gone, but the Problem Hasn't disappeared." CBS News (June 12, 2020). https://www.cbsnews.com/news/redlining-what-is-history-mike-bloomberg-comments/.

Brown, DeNeen L. "Martin Luther King Jr. Was Stabbed by a Deranged Woman. At 29, He Almost Died." *The Washington Post* (Jan. 21, 2019). https://www.washingtonpost.com/history/2019/01/21/martin-luther-king-jr-was-stabbed-by-deranged-woman-he-almost-died/.

"Brown v. Board of Education." History.com (April 8, 2020). https://www.history.com/topics/black-history/brown-v-board-of-education-of-topeka.

"Brown v. Board of Education of Topeka (2)." *Oyez*. https://www.oyez.org/cases/1940-1955/349us294.

Bryant, Nick. "Martin Luther King and the Race Riot That Never Was." BBC News (Aug. 25, 2013). Martin Luther King and the race riot that never was - BBC News.

Campbell, Molly. "Genotype vs. Phenotype: Examples and Definitions." *Genomics Research from Technology Networks* (Apr. 18, 2019). https://www.technologynetworks.com/genomics/articles/genotype-vs-phenotype-examples-and-definitions-318446.

CBS News. "Police in the U.S. Killed 164 Black People in the First 8 Months of 2020. These Are Their Names." https://www.cbsnews.com/pictures/black-people-killed-by-police-in-the-u-s-in-2020/.

Chou, Vivian. "How Science and Genetics Are Reshaping the Race Debate of the 21st Century," *Science in the News* (harvard.edu).

"Civil War." History.com (June 23, 2020). https://www.history.com/topics/american-civil-war/american-civil-war-history.

Clark, Alexis. "Tulsa's 'Black Wall Street' Flourished as a Self-Contained Hub in Early 1900s," History.com (Jan. 2, 2020). https://www.history.com/news/black-wall-street-tulsa-race-massacre.

Coen, Ross. "Sundown Towns." *BlackPast* (August 23, 2020). https://www.blackpast.org/african-american-history/sundown-towns/.

"Compromise of 1850." History.com (Feb. 10, 2020). https://www.history.com/topics/abolitionist-movement/compromise-of-1850.

"Compromise of 1877." History.com. https://www.history.com/topics/us-presidents/compromise-of-1877.

"Congress Abolishes the African Slave Trade." History.com (Dec. 4, 2020). Congress abolishes the African slave trade - HISTORY.

Copeland, Libby. "You Can Learn a Lot About Yourself From a DNA Test. Here's What Your Genes Cannot Tell You." *Time Magazine* (March 2, 2020). https://time.com/5783784/dna-testing-genetics/.

Davis, F. James. "Who Is Black? One Nation's Definition," Frontline. https://www.pbs.org/wgbh/pages/frontline/shows/jefferson/mixed/onedrop.html.

DeWeerdt, Sarah E. "What's a Genome?" *Genome News Network* (Jan. 15, 2003). https://www.genomenewsnetwork.org/resources/whats_a_genome/Chp1_1_1.shtml#genome1.

DeWeerdt, Sarah E. "Genome Variations." *Genome News Network* (Jan. 15, 2003). http://www.genomenewsnetwork.org/resources/whats_a_genome/Chp4_1.shtml.

"Dred Scott Case." History.com (Aug. 26, 2020). https://www.history.com/topics/black-history/dred-scott-case.

Du Bois, W. E. Burghardt. The Souls of Black Folk. Chicago, 1903. Cited in "W.E.B. Du Bois Critiques Booker T. Washington." *History Matters*. http://historymatters.gmu.edu/d/40.

Earley, P. Christopher and Elaine Mosakowski. "Cultural Intelligence." *Harvard Business Review* (Oct. 2004). https://hbr.org/2004/10/cultural-intelligence.

"Emancipation and Reconstruction." History.com (Nov. 2, 2020). https://www.history.com/topics/american-civil-war/reconstruction.

"Emancipation Proclamation." Africans in America. PBS. https://www.pbs.org/wgbh/aia/part4/4h1549.html.

"Emancipation Proclamation." History.com (Sept. 18, 2020). https://www.history.com/topics/american-civil-war/emancipation-proclamation.

"Eugenics." History.com. https://www.history.com/topics/germany/eugenics.

Featherstone, Thomas. "No Greater Calling: The Life of Walter P. Reuther." *Wayne State University Library*. http://reuther100.wayne.edu/bio.php?pg=4.

"First Enslaved Africans Arrive in Jamestown, Setting the Stage for Slavery in North America." History.com. https://www.history.com/this-day-in-history/first-african-slave-ship-arrives-jamestown-colony.

Foner, Eric. "Reconstruction." Britannica.com (Sept. 10, 2020). https://www.britannica.com/event/Reconstruction-United-States-history.

"Freedmen's Bureau." History.com (Oct. 3, 2018). https://www.history.com/topics/black-history/freedmens-bureau#:~:text=The%20Freedmen's%20Bureau%2C%20formally%20known,aftermath%20of%20the%Civil%20War.

Gould, Stephen Jay. "The Geometer of Race." *Discover* (Nov. 1, 1994). https://www.discovermagazine.com/mind/the-geometer-of-race.

Hanna, Charles W. *African American Recipients of the Medal of Honor*. Jefferson, NC: McFarland & Company, 2002.

Harlan, Louis R. ed. The Booker T. Washington Papers. Vol. 3. Urbana: University of Illinois Press, 1974. pp. 583-587. Cited in "Booker T. Washington Delivers the 1895 Atlanta Compromise Speech." *History Matters*. http://historymatters.gmu.edu/d/39/.

https://innocenceproject.org/.

https://www.youtube.com/watch?v=tkpUyB2xgTM.

Huddleston, Tom Jr. "Juneteenth: The 155-Year-Old Holiday's History Explained." CNBC.com (June 17, 2020). https://www.cnbc.com/2020/06/15/what-is-juneteenth-holidays-history-explained.html.

"I Have a Dream." *I Have a Dream: Writings and Speeches That Changed the World. Martin Luther King, Jr.*, edited by James M. Washington (New York: HarperCollins, 1986, 1992).

Ignatiev, Noel. *How the Irish Became White.* New York: Routledge, 1994.

"Jackson, Jimmie Lee: Biography," Stanford University. *Martin Luther King, Jr. Research and Education Institute.* https://kinginstitute.stanford.edu/encyclopedia/jackson-jimmie-lee.

"Jim Crow Laws." History.com (Dec. 2, 2020). https://www.history.com/topics/early-20th-century-us/jim-crow-laws.

Jones, Jonathan. "'Some of the Most Appalling Images Ever Created'—I Am Ashurbanipal Review." *The Guardian* (Nov. 5, 2018). https://www.theguardian.com/artanddesign/2018/nov/06/i-am-ashurbanipal-review-british-museum.

Kansas-Nebraska Act." History.com (Aug. 27, 2019). https://www.history.com/topics/19th-century/kansas-nebraska-act.

Kaufman, Michael T. "Robert K. Merton, Versatile Sociologist and Father of the Focus Group, Dies at 92." *New York Times* (Feb. 24, 2003). https://www.nytimes.com/2003/02/24/nyregion/robert-k-merton-versatile-sociologist-and-father-of-the-focus-group-dies-at-92.html.

Kelley, Peter. "Documents That Changed the World: The Declaration of Independence's Deleted Passage on Slavery, 1776." *UW News* (Feb. 25, 2016). https://www.washington.edu/news/2016/02/25/documents-that-changed-the-world-the-declaration-of-independences-deleted-passage-on-slavery-1776/#:~:text=The%20deleted%20words%20%E2%80%94%20beginning%20with,his%20participation%20in%20and%20perpetuation.

"Kenneth and Mamie Clark Doll." *National Park Service* (April 10, 2015). https://www.nps.gov/brvb/learn/historyculture/clarkdoll.htm.

Kindig, Jessie. "March on Washington Movement (1941–1947)." *BlackPast* (Dec. 6, 2007). https://www.blackpast.org/african-american-history/march-washington-movement-1941-1947/.

Klein, Christopher. "How Selma's 'Bloody Sunday' Became a Turning Point in the Civil Rights Movement. History.

com (July 18, 2020). https://www.history.com/news/
selma-bloody-sunday-attack-civil-rights-movement.

"Ku Klux Klan." History.com (Nov. 2, 2020). https://www.history.com/
topics/reconstruction/ku-klux-klan.

Lartey, Jamiles and Sam Morris. "How White Americans Used Lynchings
to Terrorize and Control Black People." *The Guardian* (April 26,
2018). https://www.theguaardian.com/us-news/2018/apr/26/
lynchings-memorial-us-south-montgomery-alabama.

"Lest We Forget: The Lynching of Will Brown, Omaha's 1919 Race
Riot." *History Nebraska Blog*. Accessed Nov. 17, 2020. https://
history.nebraska.gov/blog/lest-we-forget-lynching-will-brown-
omaha%E2%80%99s-1919-race-riot.

"Letter to Albert G. Hodges." *Abraham Lincoln Online*. http://www.
abrahamlincolnonline.org/lincoln/speeches/hodges.htm.

"Letter to Emmett C. Hoctor From Anonymous, Omaha, Nebraska,
May 25, 1919." Copy in possession of Orville D. Menard. https://
history.nebraska.gov/sites/history.nebraska.gov/files/doc/publications/
NH2010Lynching. pdf.

Lieutenant Colonel Jeffrey A. Calvert. "The Occupation of the South."
Army Heritage Center Foundation. https://www.armyheritage.org/
soldier-stories-information/the-occupation-of-the-south/.

"Lincoln's Evolving Thoughts on Slavery, and Freedom." Oct. 11,
2010. From NPR Interview With Eric Foner. *The Fiery Trial:
Abraham Lincoln and American Slavery* (New York: W.W. Norton
& Company, 2010). https://www.npr.org/2010/10/11/130489804/
lincolns-evolving-thoughts-on-slavery-and-freedom.

Loewen, James W. *Sundown Towns: A Dimension of American Racism*. New
York: the New Press, 2005.

"Lynching in America: Confronting the Legacy of Racial Terror." *Equal
Justice Initiative*, 2017. https://lynchinginamerica.eji.org/report/.

McKenna, Amy. "Black Code." Britannica.com. (Aug. 20, 2019). https://
www.britannica.com/topic/black-code.

McNeill, Leila. "How a Psychologist's Work on Race Identity Helped
Overturn School Segregation in 1950s America." *Smithsonian
Magazine* (Oct. 26, 2017). https://www.smithsonianmag.com/science-
nature/psychologist-work-racial-identity-helped-overturn-school-
segregation-180966934/.

Mai, Lina. "'I Had a Right to Be at Central': Remembering Little Rock's
Integration Battle." *Time* (Sept. 22, 2017). https://time.com/4948704/
little-rock-nine-anniversary/.

Lewis, C. S., *The Weight of Glory*. New York: HarperCollins, 1949.

"Manifest Destiny." *U.S. History*. https://www.ushistory.org/us/29.asp.

"Mary Turner, Pregnant, Lynched in Georgia for Publicly Criticizing Husband's Lynching." *Equal Justice Initiative*. https://calendar.eji.org/racial-injustice/may/19.

Merton, Robert K. *Sociological Ambivalence and Other Essays*. New York: The Free Press, 1976.

Michals, Debra, ed. "Fannie Lou Hamer." *National Women's History Museum*, 2017. https://www.womenshistory.org/education-resources/biographies/fannie-lou-hamer.

Michals, Debra. "Ruby Bridges." *National Women's History Museum*, 2015. https://www.womenshistory.org/education-resources/biographies/ruby-bridges.

Miller, Melissa T. "The Tuskegee Airmen." Military.com. https://military.com/history/the-tuskegee-airmen.html.

"Missouri Compromise." History.com (Nov. 4, 2019). https://www.history.com/topics/abolitionist-movement/missouri-compromise.

Mitchell, Paul Wolff and Janet Monge. "A New Take on the 19th-Century Skull Collection of Samuel Morton," *Science Daily* (Oct. 4, 2018). https://www.sciencedaily.com/releases/2018/10/181004143943.htm.

Nature Education. "Phenotype/phenotypes." Scitable. https://www.nature.com/scitable/definition/phenotype-phenotypes-35/.

"Niagara Movement." History.com. https://www.history.com/topics/black-history/niagara-movement.

"1921 Tulsa Race Massacre." *Tulsa Historical Society and Museum*. https://www.tulsahistory.org/exhibit/1921-tulsa-race-massacre/#flexible-content.

Pauls, Elizabeth Prine. "Trail of Tears." *Encyclopaedia Britannica*. https://www.britannica.com/event/Trail-of-Tears.

"Personal Self-Assessment of Anti-Bias Behavior." *Anti-Defamation League*, 2007. https://www.adl.org/sites/default/files/documents/assets/pdf/education-outreach/Personal-Self-Assessment-of-Anti-Bias-Behavior.pdf.

"Plessy v. Ferguson." History.com. https://www.history.com/topics/black-history/plessy-v-ferguson.

Pruitt, Sarah. "5 things You May Not Know about Abraham Lincoln, slavery and Emancipation." History.com (June 23, 2020). https://www.history.com/news/5-things-you-may-not-know-about-lincoln-slavery-and-emancipation.

"Reeb, James." *Stanford University. Martin Luther King, Jr., Research and Education Institute.* https://kinginstitute.stanford.edu/encyclopedia/reeb-james.

Rho, Eunice Hyon Min. "Remembering Dr. King's Defense of Voting Rights." ACLU.org. (Jan. 16, 2012). Remembering Dr. King's Defense of Voting Rights | American Civil Liberties Union (aclu.org)

Rothstein, Richard, *The Color of Law: A Forgotten History of How Our government Segregated America.* New York: Liveright Publishing, 2017.

"Ruby Bridges," *Biography* (June 22, 2020). https://www.biography.com/activist/ruby-bridges.

Rutherford, Alexandra. "Developmental Psychologist, Starting From Strengths." Cited in McNeill, Ibid.

Schjonberg, Mary Frances. "Remembering Jonathan Daniels 50 Years After His Martyrdom." *Episcopal News Service* (Aug. 13, 2015). https://www.episcopalnewsservice.org/2015/08/13/remembering-jonathan-daniels-50-years-after-his-martyrdom/, and "Jonathan Daniels, Civil Rights Hero." *Virginia Military Institute.* https://www.vmi.edu/archives/genealogy-biography-alumni/featured-historical-biographies/jonathan-daniels-civil-rights-hero/.

"(1776) The Deleted Passage of the Declaration of Independence." *BlackPast* (Aug. 10, 2009). https://www.blackpast.org/african-american-history/declaration-independence-and-debate-over-slavery/.

"Selma to Montgomery March." *Stanford University. Martin Luther King, Jr. Research and Education Institute.* https://kinginstitute.stanford.edu/encyclopedia/selma-montgomery-march.

Simba, M. "The Three-Fifths Clause of the United States Constitution (1787)." *BlackPast* (Oct. 3, 2014). https://www.blackpast.org/african-american-history/three-fifths-clause-united-states-constitution-1787/.

"The Berlin Olympics." *The History Place.* Accessed Dec. 3, 2020. https://www.historyplace.com/worldwar2/triumph/tr-olympics.htm.

"The Civil Rights Act of 1875." *History, Art & Archives. United States House of Representatives.* https://history.house.gov/Historical-Highlights/1851-1900/The-Civil-Rights-Act-of-1875/ and "Civil Rights Act of 1875 Declared Unconstitutional." *Annenberg Classroom.* https://www.annenbergclassroom.org/timeline_event/civil-rights-act-of-1875-declared-unconstitutional/.

"The Civil Rights Bill of 1866." *History, Art & Archives. United States House of Representatives.* https://history.house.gov/Historical-Highlights/1851-1900/The-Civil-Rights-Bill-of-1866/.

"The 1788 Dolben Act." *Spartacus Educational.* https://spartacus-educational.com/REdolbenAct.htm.

"13th Amendment." History.com (June 9, 2020). 13th Amendment - HISTORY

"Top 100 Speeches." *American Rhetoric.* https://www.americanrhetoric.com/speeches/mlkihaveadream.htm.

"Trail of Tears." History.com (July 7, 2020). https://www.history.com/topics/native-american-history/trail-of-tears.

"Ulysses S. Grant." History.com (March 30, 2020). https://www.history.com/topics/us-presidents/ulysses-s-grant-1.

Urofsky, Melvin I. "Civil Rights Cases." *Britannica* (Oct. 8, 2020). https://www.britannica.com/topic/Civil-Rights-Cases.

"Viola Gregg Liuzzo Biography." *Biography* (Nov. 19, 2020). https://www. Biography.com/activist/viola-gregg-liuzzo.

"Viola Liuzzo, killed by the Klan, was the only white woman to die in the civil rights movement" *The Washington Post.*

"Voting Rights Act of 1965." *Stanford University. Martin Luther King, Jr. Research and Education Institute.* https://kinginstitute.stanford.edu/liberation-curriculum/lesson-plans/activities/chicago

White, Walter. "The Eruption of Tulsa." *Nation* (June 29, 1921). Cited in "Introduction of Hannibal B. Johnson." *Black Wall Street 100* (Fort Worth: Eakin Press, 2020).

Woodward, C. Vann. Plessy v. Ferguson." *American Heritage,* Vol. 15, Issue 3, 1964. https://www.americanheritage.com/plessy-v-ferguson#1.

Worrall, Simon. Quoting British Geneticist Adam Rutherford in "Why Race Is Not a Thing, According to Genetics," *National Geographic* (Oct. 14, 2017). https://www.nationalgeographic.com/news/2017/10/genetics-history-race-neanderthal-rutherford/.

Supplemental Reading

For further information on the topic of race, the author recommends reading the following books:

Alexander, Michelle. *The New Jim Crow: Mass Incarceration in the Age of Colorblindness.* New York: The New Press, 2011.

Buell, Denise Kimber. *Why This New Race: Ethnic Reasoning in Early Christianity.* New York: Columbia University Press, 2005.

Desmond, Matthew and Mustafa Emirbayer. *Racial Domination. Racial Progress: The Sociology of Race in America.* New York: McGraw Hill, 2010.

Elmer, Duane. *Cross-Cultural Connections: Stepping Out and Fitting in Around the World.* Downers Grove, Ill.: InterVarsity Press, 2002.

Emerson, Michael O. and Christian Smith. *Divided by Faith: Evangelical Religion and the Problem of Race in America.* New York: Oxford University Press, 2000.*

Greenway, Roger S. and Timothy M. Monsma. *Cities: Missions' New Frontier.* Grand Rapids: Baker Book House, 1990.

Jenkins, Willie James. *The Christian Imagination: Theology and the Origins of Race.* New Haven, CT: Yale University Press, 2011.*

Kendi, Ibram X. *Stamped From the Beginning: The Definitive History of Racist Ideas in America.* Bold Type Books, 2017.*

Parrillo, Vincent N. *Diversity in America, Third Edition.* Los Angeles: Pine Forge Press, 2009.

Priest, Robert J. and Alvaro L. Nieves. *This Side of Heaven: Race, Ethnicity, and Christian Faith.* New York: Oxford University Press, 2007.

Rothstein, Richard. *Color of Law: A Forgotten History of How Our Government Segregated America.* New York: Liveright Publishing Corporation, 2017.*

Tisby, Jemar. *How to Fight Racism: Courageous Christianity and the Journey Toward Racial Justice.* Grand Rapids: Zondervan, 2021.*

These titles may also be obtained through Amazon's Audible Audiobooks.